# Little Journeys To The Homes Of...: Eminent Painters...

Elbert Hubbard, Roycroft Shop

**Nabu Public Domain Reprints:**

You are holding a reproduction of an original work published before 1923 that is in the public domain in the United States of America, and possibly other countries. You may freely copy and distribute this work as no entity (individual or corporate) has a copyright on the body of the work. This book may contain prior copyright references, and library stamps (as most of these works were scanned from library copies). These have been scanned and retained as part of the historical artifact.

This book may have occasional imperfections such as missing or blurred pages, poor pictures, errant marks, etc. that were either part of the original artifact, or were introduced by the scanning process. We believe this work is culturally important, and despite the imperfections, have elected to bring it back into print as part of our continuing commitment to the preservation of printed works worldwide. We appreciate your understanding of the imperfections in the preservation process, and hope you enjoy this valuable book.

# Little Journeys

## to the Homes of

### Eminent Painters

Book One

**MIRIAM EDITION**

Written by Elbert Hubbard
and done into a Book by The
Roycrofters at their Shop, at
East Aurora, New York, MCMVIII

Copyright, 1911
By Elbert Hubbard

## CONTENTS

| | |
|---|---|
| MICHELANGELO | 5 |
| REMBRANDT | 39 |
| RUBENS | 77 |
| MEISSONIER | 115 |
| TITIAN | 141 |
| ANTHONY VAN DYCK | 165 |

86 X 790   MICHELANGELO

How can that be, lady, which all men learn
By long experience? Shapes that seem alive,
Wrought in hard mountain marble, will survive
Their maker, whom the years to dust return!
Thus to effect, cause yields. Art hath her turn,
And triumphs over Nature. I, who strive with sculpture,
Know this well: her wonders live
In spite of time and death, those tyrants stern.
So I can give long life to both of us
In either way, by color or by stone,
Making the semblance of thy face and mine.
Centuries hence when both are buried,
Thus thy beauty and my sadness shall be shown,
And men shall say, "For her 't was wise to pine."
—Sonnets of Michelangelo.

# MICHELANGELO

"CALL me by my pet name," wrote Elizabeth Barrett Browning, in one of those incomparable sonnets of which the Portuguese never heard. And the task yet remains for some psychologist to tell us why, when we wish to bestow the highest honor, coupled with familiar affection, we call the individual by a given name.

Young men and maidens will understand my allusion; and I hope this book will not suffer the dire fate of falling into the hands of any one who has forgotten the days of his youth.

In addressing the one we truly revere, we drop all prefix and titles. Soldiers marching under the banner of a beloved leader ever have for him a name of their own. What honor and trust were once compressed into the diminutive, "Little Corporal," or Kipling's "Bobs"; or to come down to something even more familiar to us, say, "Old Abe" and "Little Phil"!

The earth is a vast graveyard where untold millions of men lie buried, but out of the myriads who pass into forgetfulness every decade, the race holds a few names embalmed in undying amber.

¶ Lovers of art, the round world over,

carry in their minds one character, so harmoniously developed on every side of his nature that we say twenty centuries have never produced his equal. We call him "Leonardo"—the one ideal man. Leonardo da Vinci was painter, poet, sculptor, architect, mathematician, politician, musician, man of science, and courtier. His disposition was so joyous, his manner so captivating, his form and countenance so beautiful, that wherever he went all things were his. And he was so well ballasted with brains, and so acute in judgment, that flattery spoiled him not. His untiring industry and transcendent talent brought him large sums of money, and he spent them like a king. So potent was his personality that wherever he made his home there naturally grew up around him a Court of Learning, and his pupils and followers were counted by the score. To the last of his long life he carried with him the bright, expectant animation of youth; and to all who knew him he was "Leonardo—the only Leonardo."

But great as was Leonardo, we call the time in which he lived, the age of Michelangelo.

When Leonardo was forty, and at the very height of his power, Michael Agnola Buonarroti, aged twenty, liberated from the block a marble Cupid that was so exquisite in its proportions that it passed for an antique, and men who looked upon it exclaimed, "Phidias!"

Michael Agnola became Michelangelo, that is to say, "Michael the Angel," in a day. The name thrown at him by an unknown admirer stuck, and in his later years when all the world called him "Angelo" he cast off the name his parents had given him and accepted the affectionate pet name that clung like the love of woman.

Michelangelo was born in a shabby little village but a few miles from Florence. In another village near by was born Leonardo. "Great men never come singly," says Emerson. And yet Angelo and Leonardo exercised no influence upon each other that we can trace. The younger man never came under the spell of the older one, but moved straight on to his destiny, showing not the slightest arc in his orbit in deference to the great luminary of his time.

The handsome Leonardo was social: he loved women, and music, and festivals, and gorgeous attire, and magnificent equipage. His life was full of color and sweeping, joyous, rainbow tints.

Michelangelo was homely in feature, and the aspect of his countenance was mutilated by a crashing blow from a rival student's mallet that flattened his nose to his face. Torrigiano lives in history for this act alone, thus proving that there are more ways than one to gain immortality.

Angelo was proud, self-centered, independent, and he sometimes lashed the critics into a buzzing, bluebottle fury by his sarcastic speech. "He affronted polite society, conformed to no one's dictates, lived like an ascetic and worked like a packmule," says a contemporary.

Vasari, who among his many other accomplishments seems to have been the Boswell of his time, compares Leonardo and Michelangelo. He says, "Angelo can do everything that Leonardo can, although he does it differently." Further, he adds, "Angelo is painter, sculptor, engineer, architect and poet." "But," adds this versatile Italian Samuel Pepys, somewhat sorrowfully, "he is not a gentleman."

It is to be regretted that Signor Vasari did not follow up his remarks with his definition of the term "gentleman."

Leonardo was more of a painter than a sculptor. His pictures are full of rollicking mirth, and the smile on the faces of his women is handed down by imitation even to this day. The joyous freedom of animal life beckons from every Leonardo canvas; and the backgrounds fade off into fleecy clouds and shadowy, dreamy, opiate odor of violets.

Michelangelo, however, is true to his own life as Leonardo was to his—for at the last the artist only reproduces himself. He never painted a laugh, for life to him was serious and full of sober purpose. We can not call his work somber—it does not depress—for it carries with it a poise and a strength that is sufficient unto itself. It is all heroic, and there is in it a subtle quality that exorcises fear and bids care begone.

¶ No man ever portrayed the human figure with the same fidelity that Angelo has. The naked Adam, when the finger of the Almighty touched him into life, gives one a thrill of health to look upon, even after these four hundred years have struggled to obliterate the lines.

His figures of women shocked the artistic sense of his time, for instead of the Greek idealization of beauty he carved the swelling muscles and revealed the articulations of form as no artist before him had ever dared. His women are never young, foolish, timid girls—they are Amazons; and his men are the kind that lead nations out of captivity. The soft, the pretty, the yielding, were far from him. There is never a suggestion of taint or double meaning; all is frank, open, generous, honest and fearless. His figures are nude, but never naked.

He began his artistic work when fourteen years old, and lived to be eighty-nine; and his years did not outlast his zeal and zest. He was above the medium size, an athlete in his lean and sinewy strength, and the whipcord quality of his body mirrored the silken strength of his will. ¶ In his old age the King arose when Michelangelo entered the Council-Chamber, and would not sit until he was seated at the right hand of the throne; the Pope would not allow him to kneel before him; when he walked through the streets of Rome the people removed their hats as he passed; and today we who gaze upon his work in the Eternal City stand uncovered.

MICHELANGELO was the firstborn in a large family. Simone Buonarroti, his father, belonged to an ebb-tide branch of the nobility that had lost everything but the memory of great ancestors turned to dust. This father had ambitions for his boy; ambitions in the line of the army or a snug office under the wing of the State, where he might, by following closely the beck and nod of the prince in power, become a magistrate or a keeper of customs.
But no boy ever disappointed a proud father more.
When great men in gilt and gold braid, with scarlet sashes across their breasts, and dangling swords that clicked and clanged on the stone pavement, strode by, rusty, dusty little Michael refused to take off his cap and wish them "Long life and God's favor," as his father ordered. Instead, he hid behind his mother's gown and made faces. His father used to say he was about as homely as he could be without making faces, and if he did n't watch out he would get his face crooked some day and could n't get it back.
Simone Buonarroti had qualities very Micawber-like mixed in his clay, and the way he cringed and crawled may have had something to do with setting the son on the other tack.
¶ The mother was only nineteen when Michael was born, and although the moralists talk much about woman's vanity and extravagance, the theory gets no backing from this quarter. She was a plain woman in appearance, quiet and self-contained, with no nerves to speak of, a sturdy physical endowment, and commonsense enough for two ❧
When scarcely out of dresses the boy began to draw pictures. He drew with charcoal on the walls, or with a stick in the

sand, and shaped curious things out of mud in the gutters.
¶ It was an age of creative art, and most of the work being in the churches the common people had their part in it. In fact, the common people were the artists. And when Simone Buonarroti found his twelve-year-old boy haunting the churches to watch the workmen, and also discovered that he was consorting with the youths who studied drawing in the atelier of Ghirlandajo, he was displeased.

Painters, to this erstwhile nobleman, were simply men in blue blouses who worked for low wages on high scaffolds, and occasionally spattered color on the good clothes of ladies and gentlemen who were beneath. He did n't really hate painters, he simply waived them; and to his mind there was no difference between an artisan and an artist.

The mother, however, took a secret pride in her boy's drawings, as mothers always do in a son's accomplishments. Doubtless she knew something of the art of decoration, too, for she had brothers who worked as day laborers on high scaffolds. Yet she did n't say much about it, for women then did n't have so much to say about anything as now ॐ ॐ But I can imagine that this good woman, as she went daily to church to pray, the year before her first child was born, watched the work of the men on the scaffolds, and observed that day by day the pictures grew; and as she looked, the sun streamed through stained windows and revealed to her the miracles of form and color, and the impressions of "The Annunciation," "Mary's Visit to Elizabeth" and "The Babe in the Manger" filled her wondering soul with thoughts and feelings too great for speech. To his mother was Michelangelo indebted for his leaning toward art 🌿 His father opposed such a plebeian bent vigorously:

"Bah! to love beautiful things is all right, but to wish to devote all of one's time to making them, just for others—ouch! it hurts me to think of it!"

The mother was lenient and said, "But if our child can not be anything more than a painter—why, we must be content, and God willing, let us hope he will be a good one."

Ghirlandajo's was practically a school where, for a consideration, boys were taught the secrets of fresco. The master always had contracts of his own on hand and by using 'prentice talent made both ends meet. Young Michael made it his lounging-place and when he strayed from home his mother always knew where to find him.

The master looked upon him as a possible pupil, and instead of ordering him away, smiled indulgently and gave him tasks of mixing colors and making simple lines. And the boy showed such zest and comprehension that in a short time he could draw free-hand with a confidence that set the brightest scholar in the background. Such a pupil, so alert, so willing, so anxious, is the joy of a teacher's heart. Ghirlandajo must have him—he would inspire the whole school!

So the master went to the father, but the father demurred, and his scruples were only overcome when Ghirlandajo offered to reverse the rule, and pay the father the sum that parents usually paid the master. A cash payment down caused pater to capitulate, and the boy went to work—aged fourteen.

# MICHELANGELO

The terms of his apprenticeship called for three years, but after he had been at work a year, the ability of the youth made such an impression on the master that he took him to Lorenzo, Lorenzo the Magnificent, who then ruled over Florence 🌸 🌸

Lorenzo had him draw a few sketches, and he was admitted to the Academy 🌸 This "Academy" was situated in the palace of Lorenzo, and in the gardens was a rich collection of antique marbles: busts, columns, and valuable fragments that had come down from the days when Pericles did for Athens what Lorenzo was then doing for Florence. The march of commerce has overrun the garden, but in the Uffizi Gallery are to be seen today most of the curios that Lorenzo collected.

By introducing the lad to Lorenzo, Ghirlandajo lost his best helper, but so unselfish was this excellent master that he seemed quite willing to forego his own profit that the boy might have the best possible advantages. And I never think of Ghirlandajo without mentally lifting my hat.

At the Academy, Michelangelo ceased to paint and draw, and devoted all his energies to modeling in clay. So intent was his application that in a few weeks he had mastered technicalities that took others years to comprehend.

One day the father came and found the boy in blouse at work with mallet and chisel on a block of marble. "And is it a stone-mason you want to make of my heir and first-born?" asked the fond father.

It was explained that there were stone-masons and stone-masons. A stone-mason of transcendent skill is a sculptor, just as a painter who can produce a beautiful picture is an artist.

Simone Buonarroti acknowledged he had never looked at it just in that way, but still he would not allow his son to remain at the trade unless—unless he himself had an office under the government.

Lorenzo gave him the desired office, and took the young stone-mason as one of the Medici family, and there the boy lived in the Palace, and Lorenzo acted toward him as though he were his son.

The favor with which he was treated excited the envy of some of the other pupils, and thus it was that in sudden wrath Torrigiano struck him that murderous blow with the mallet. Torrigiano paid for his fierce temper, not only by expulsion from the Academy, but by banishment from Florence ❧ ❧

Michelangelo was the brightest of the hundred young men who worked and studied at the Medici palace.

But when this head scholar was eighteen Lorenzo died. The son of Lorenzo continued his father's work in a feeble way, for Piero de' Medici was a good example of the fact that great men seldom reproduce themselves after the flesh. Piero had about as much comprehension of the beautiful as the elder Buonarroti. He thought that all these young men who were being educated at the Academy would eventually be valuable adjuncts to the State, and as such it was a good scheme to give each a trade—besides, it kept them off the street; and then the work was amusing, a diversion to the nobility when time hung heavy.

Once there came a heavy snowstorm, and snow being an unusual thing in Florence, Piero called a lot of his friends together in the gardens, and summoning Michelangelo, ordered him to make a snow image for the amusement of the guests, just as Piero at other times had a dog jump through a hoop.

"What shall it be?" asked Michelangelo.

"Oh, anything you please," replied Piero; "only don't keep us waiting here in the cold all day!"

Young Angelo cast one proud look of contempt toward the group and set to work making a statue. In ten minutes he had formed a satyr that bore such a close resemblance to Piero that the guests roared with laughter. "That will do," called Piero; "like Deity, you make things in your own image." Some of the company tossed silver coin at the young man, but he let the money lie where it fell.

Michael at this time was applying himself to the study of anatomy, and giving his attention to literature under the tutorship of the famous poet and scholar, Poliziano, who resided at the court.

So filled was the young man's mind with his work that he was blind to the discontent arising in the State. To the young, governments and institutions are imperishable. Piero by his selfish whims had been digging the grave of the Medici. From sovereignty they were flung into exile. The palace was sacked, the beautiful gardens destroyed, and Michelangelo, being regarded as one of the family, was obliged to flee for his life. He arrived in Bologna penniless and friendless, and applied to a sculptor for work.

"What can you do?" the old sculptor asked. For answer, Michelangelo silently took a crayon and sketched a human hand on the wall. Marvelous were the lines! The master put his arms around the boy and kissed his cheek.

This new-found friend took him into his house, and placed him at his own table. Michelangelo was led into the library and workrooms, and told that all was his to use as he liked.

¶ The two years he remained at Bologna were a great benefit to the young man. The close contact with cultured minds, and the encouragement he received, spurred his spirit to increased endeavor. It was here that he began that exquisite statue of a Cupid that passed for an antique, and found its way into the cabinet of the Duchess of Mantua.

¶ Before long the discovery was made that the work was done by a young man only a little past twenty, and Cardinal San Giorgio sent a message inviting him to Rome.

ROME had long been the Mecca of the boy's ambitions, and he joyously accepted the invitation.

At Rome he was lodged in the Vatican, and surrounded by that world of the beautiful, he went seriously about his life's work.

The Church must have the credit for being the mother of modern art. Not only did she furnish the incentive, but she supplied the means. She gave security from the eternal grind of material wants and offered men undying fame as reward for noble effort.

The letter of religion was nothing to Michelangelo, but the eternal spirit of truth that broods over and beyond all forms and ceremonies touched his soul. His heart was filled with the poetry of pagan times. The gods of ancient Greece on high Olympus for him still sang and feasted, still lived and loved ✄ ✄

But to the art of the Church he devoted his time and talents. He considered himself a priest and servant to the cause of Christ ✄ ✄

Established at Rome in the palace of the Pope, Michelangelo felt secure. He knew his power. He knew he could do work that would for generations move men to tears, and in his prophetic soul was a feeling that his name would be inseparably linked with Rome. His wanderings and buffetings were things of the past—he was necessary to the Church, and his position was now secure and safe. The favor of princes lasts but for a day, but the Church is eternal. The Church should be his bride, to her and to her alone would he give his passionate soul. Thus mused Michelangelo, aged twenty-two.

His first work at Rome was a statue of Bacchus, done it seems for an exercise to give Cardinal Giorgio a taste of his quality, just as he had drawn the human hand on the wall for his Bologna protector; for this fine and lofty pride in his power was a thing that clung to Michelangelo from rosy youth to hoary age.

The "Bacchus," which is now in the National Museum at Florence, added to his reputation; and the little world of art, whose orbit was the Vatican, anxiously awaited a more serious attempt, just as we crane our necks when the great violinist about to play awakens expectation by a few preliminary flourishes.

His first great work at Rome was the "Pieta." We see it today in Saint Peter's at the first chapel to the right as we enter, in a long row of commonplace marbles, in all its splendid beauty and strength. It represents the Mother of Christ, supporting in her arms the dead body just after it was lowered from the cross. In most of Michelangelo's work there is a heroic quality in the figures and a muscular strength that in a degree detracts from the spirit of sympathy that might otherwise come over us. It is admiration that seizes us, not sympathy ✤ But this early work is the flower of Michelangelo's genius, round and full and complete. The later work may be different, but it is not better.

When this group was unveiled in Fourteen Hundred Ninety-eight it was the sensation of the year. Old and young, rich and poor, learned and unlearned, flocked to see it, and the impression it made was most profound. If the Catholic Church has figured on the influence of statuary and painting on the superstitious, as has been tauntingly said, she has reckoned well. The story of steadfast love and loyalty is masterly told in that first great work of Michelangelo. The artist himself often mingled with the crowds that surrounded his speaking marble, and the people who knelt before it assured him by their reverence that his hand had wrought well. And once he heard two able doctors disputing as to who the artist was. They were lavish in their praise, and one insisted that the work was done by the great sculptor at Bologna, and he named the master who had befriended Michelangelo. The artist stood by and heard the argument put forth that no mere youth could conceive such a work, much less execute it.

That night he stole into the church and by the wan light of a lantern carved his name deep on the girdle of the Virgin, and there do we read it today. The pride of the artist, however, afterward took another turn, for he never thereafter placed his name on a piece. "My work is unlike any other —no lover of the beautiful can mistake it," he proudly said.

¶ He worked away with untiring industry and the Church paid him well. But many of his pieces have been carried from Rome, and as they were not signed and scores of imitations sprang up, it can not always be determined now what is his work and what not. He toiled alone, and allowed no 'prentice hand to use the chisel, and unlike the sculptors of our day, did not work from a clay model, but fell upon the block direct. "I caught sight of Michelangelo at work, but could not approach for the shower of chips," writes a visitor at Rome in the year Fifteen Hundred One.

**P**ERFECT peace is what Michelangelo expected to find in the palace of the Pope. Later he came to know that life is unrest, and its passage at best a zigzag course, that only straightens to a direct line when viewed across the years. If a man does better work than his fellows he must pay the penalty. Personality is an offense.

In Rome there was a small army of painters and sculptors, each eager and anxious for the sole favor of the powers. They quibbled, quarreled, bribed, cajoled, and even fair women used their influence with cardinals and bishops in favor of this artist or that.

Michelangelo was never a favorite in society; simpering beauty peeked at him from behind feather fans and made jokes concerning his appearance. Yet Walter Pater thought he found evidence that at this time Michelangelo was beloved by a woman, and that the artist reproduced her face and form, and indirectly pictured her in poems. In feature she was as plain as he; but her mind matched his, and was of a cast too high and excellent to allow him to swerve from his high ideals. Yet the love ended unhappily, and in some mysterious way gave a tinge of melancholy and a secret spring of sorrow to the whole long life of the artist.

Jealous competitors made their influence felt. Michelangelo found his work relegated to corners and his supplies cut short ✣ ✣

At this time an invitation came from Florence for him to come and make use of a gigantic block of marble that had lain there at the city gate, blackening in the dirt, for a century ✣ ✣

The Florence that had banished him, now begged him to come back.

"Those who once leave Florence always sigh to return," says Dante. He returned, and at once began work on the "David." The result was the heroic statue that stood for three hundred years at the entrance to the Palazzo Vecchio, only a hundred feet from where Savonarola was hanged and burned. The "David" is now in the Belle d' Arte, and if the custodian will allow you to climb up on a ladder you will see that the top of the head shows the rough unfinished slab, just as it was taken from the quarry. Any one but a master would have finished the work.

This magnificent statue took nearly two years to complete. As a study of growing youth, boldly recognizing all that is awkward and immature, it has never ceased to cause wordy warfare to reign in the camp of the critics. "The feet, hands and head are all too large," the Athenians say. But linger around the "old swimmin'-hole" any Summer day, and you will see tough, bony, muscular boys that might have served as a model for the "David."

The heads of statues made by the Greeks are small in proportion to the body. The "Gladiator" wears a Number Six hat, and the "Discobolus" one size smaller; yet the figures represent men weighing one hundred and eighty pounds each. The Greeks aimed to satisfy the eye, and as the man is usually seen clothed, they reduced the size of the head when they showed the nude figure.

But Michelangelo was true to Nature, and the severest criticism ever brought against him is that he is absolutely loyal to truth. He was the first man ever to paint or model the slim, slender form of a child that has left its round baby shape behind and is shooting up like a lily-stalk. A nude, hardy boy six years old reveals ankle-bones, kneecap, sharp hips, ribs, collar-bone and shoulder-blade with startling fidelity. And why, being Nature's work, it is any less lovely than a condition of soft, cushioned adipose, we must let the critics tell, but Michelangelo thought it was n't.

From Fourteen Hundred Ninety-six, when Michelangelo first arrived in Rome, to Fifteen Hundred Four, he worked at nothing but sculpture. But now a change came over his restless spirit, for an invitation had come from the Gonfaloniere of Florence to decorate one of the rooms of the Town Hall, in competition with Leonardo da Vinci—the only Leonardo.

He painted that strong composition showing Florentine soldiers bathing in the Arno. The scene depicts the surprise of the warriors as a trumpet sounds, calling them to battle with the enemy that is near at hand. The subject was chosen because it gave opportunity for exploiting the artist's marvelous knowledge of anatomy. Thirty figures are shown in various attitudes. Nearly all are nude, and as they scramble up the bank, buckling on their armor as they rush forward, eager for the fight, we see the wild, splendid swell of muscle and warm, tense, pulsing flesh. As an example of Michelangelo's consummate knowledge of form it was believed to be his finest work.

But it did not last long; the jealous Bandinelli made a strong bid for fame by destroying it. And thus do Bandinelli and

Torregiano go clattering down the corridors of time hand in hand. Yet we know what the picture was, for various men who saw it recorded their impressions; but although many of the younger artists of Italy flocked to Florence to see it, and many copied it, only one copy has come down to us—the one in the collection of the Earl of Leicester, at Holkham.
¶ So even beautiful Florence could not treat her gifted son with impartiality, and when a call came from Pope Julius the Second, who had been elected in Fifteen Hundred Three, to return to Rome, the summons was promptly obeyed.

JULIUS was one of the most active and vigorous rulers the earth has known. He had positive ideas on many subjects and like Napoleon "could do the thinking for a world."

The first work he laid out for Michelangelo was a tomb, three stories high, with walls eighteen feet thick at the base, surrounded with numerous bas-reliefs and thirty heroic statues. It was to be a monument on the order of those worked out by the great Rameses, only incorporating the talent of Greece with that of ancient and modern Rome.

Michelangelo spent nearly a year at the Carrara quarries, getting out materials and making plans for forwarding the scheme. But gradually it came over him that the question of economy, which was deeply rooted in the mind of Julius, forbade the completion of such a gigantic and costly work. Had Julius given Michelangelo "carte-blanche" orders on the treasury, and not meddled with the plans, this surpassing piece of architecture might have found form. But the fiery Julius, aged seventy-four, was influenced by the architect Bramante to demand from Michelangelo a bill of expense and definite explanation as to details.

Very shortly after, Michelangelo quit work and sent a note to the Pope to the effect that the tomb was in the mountain of Carrara, with many beautiful statues, and if he wanted them he had better look for some one to get them out. As for himself, his address was Florence.

The Pope sent couriers after him, one after another until five had been despatched, but neither pleading, bribes nor threats could induce him to return.

As the scientist constructs the extinct animal from a thighbone, so we can guess the grandeur of what the tomb might have been from the single sample that has come down to us. The one piece of work that was completed for this tomb is the statue of "Moses." If the reputation of Michelangelo rested upon nothing else than this statue, it would be sufficient for undying fame. The "Moses" probably is better known than any other piece of Michelangelo's work. Copies of it exist in all important galleries; there are casts of it in fifty different museums in America, and pictures of it are numberless. There it stands in the otherwise obscure church of Saint Pietro in Vincolo today, one hand grasping the flowing beard, and the other sustaining the tables of the law—majesty, strength, wisdom beaming in every line. As Mr. Symonds has said, "It reveals the power of Pope Julius and Michelangelo fused into a Jove."

And so the messengers and messages were in vain, and even when the Pope sent an order to the Gonfaloniere Soderini, the actual ruler of Florence, to return the artist on pain of displeasure, the matter still rested—Michelangelo said he was neither culprit nor slave, and would live where he wished.

¶ At length the matter got so serious that it threatened the political peace of Florence, and in the goodly company of cardinals, bishops and chief citizens, Michelangelo was induced to go to Bologna and make peace with the Pope.

¶ His first task now was a bronze statue of Julius, made, it is stated, as a partial reproduction of the "Moses." Descriptions of it declare it was even finer than the "Moses," but alas! it only endured four years, for a mob evolved it into a cannon to shoot stones, and at the same time ousted Julius from Bologna.

Michelangelo very naturally seconded the anathematization of the Bolognese by Julius, not so much for the insult to the Pope as for the wretched lack of taste they had shown in destroying a work of art. Had they left the beautiful statue there on its pedestal, Bologna would now on that account alone be a place of pilgrimage. The cannon they made is lost and forgotten—buried deep in the sand by its own weight—for Mein Herr Krupp can make cannon; but, woe betide us! who can make a statue such as Michelangelo made?

¶ Michelangelo now followed the Pope to Rome and began a work that none other dare attempt, but which today excites the jealous admiration of every artist soul who views it—the ceiling of the Sistine Chapel. Ghirlandajo, Perugino, Botticelli and Luca Signorelli had worked on the walls with good effect, but to lie on one's back and paint overhead so as to bring out a masterly effect when viewed from seventy feet below was something they dare not attempt. Michelangelo put up his scaffolds, drew designs, and employed the best fresco artists in Italy to fill in the color. But as they used their brushes he saw that the designs became enfeebled under their attempts—they did not grasp the conception—and in wrath he discharged them all. He then obliterated all they had done, and shutting out the ceiling from every one but himself, worked alone. Often for days he would not leave the building, for fear some one would meddle with the work. He drew up food by a string and slept on the scaffold without changing his clothes.

After a year of intense application, no one but the artist had viewed the work. The Pope now demanded that he should be allowed to see it. A part of the scaffolding was struck, and the delight of the old Pope was unbounded. This was in Fifteen Hundred Nine, but the completed work was not shown to the public until All Souls' Day, Fifteen Hundred Twelve ❧ ❧

The guides at the Vatican tell us this ceiling was painted in twenty-two months, but the letters of Michelangelo, recently published, show that he worked on it over four years ❧ ❧

It contains over three hundred figures, all larger than life, and some are fifteen feet long. A complete description of the work Michelangelo did in this private chapel of the Pope would require a book, and in fact several books have been written with this ceiling as a subject. The technical obstacles to overcome in painting scenes and figures on an overhead surface can only be appreciated by those who have tried it. We can better appreciate the difficulties when we think that in order even to view the decorations with satisfaction, large mirrors must be used, or one must lie prone on his back. In the ability to foreshorten and give harmonious perspective—supplying the effect of motion, distance, upright movement, coming toward you or moving away—all was worked out in this historic chapel in a way that has excited the wondering admiration of artists for three hundred years.

¶ When the scaffolding was at last removed the artist thought for a time he had done his last work. The unnatural positions he had been obliged to take had so strained the muscles of his neck that on the street he had often to look straight up at the sky to rest himself, and things on a straight line in front he could not distinguish. Eyes, muscles, hands, refused to act normally.

"My life is there on the ceiling of the Chapel of Sixtus," he said ♣ ♣

He was then thirty-nine years old.

Fifty eventful years of life and work were yet before him.

# MICHELANGELO

WHEN Pope Julius died in Fifteen Hundred Thirteen, Leo the Tenth, a son of Lorenzo the Magnificent, was called to take his place. We might suppose that Leo would have remembered with pride the fact that it was his father who gave Michelangelo his first start in life, and have treated the great artist in the way Lorenzo would, were he then alive. But the retiring, abstemious habits of Michelangelo did not appeal to Leo. The handsome and gracious Raphael was his favorite, and at the expense of Michelangelo, Raphael was petted, feted and advanced. Hence arose that envious rivalry between these two great men, which reveals each in a light far from pleasant—just as if Rome were not big enough for both.

The pontificate of Leo the Tenth lasted just ten years. On account of the lack of encouragement Michelangelo received, it seems the most fruitless season of his whole life.

Clement the Seventh, another member of the Medici family, succeeded Leo. Clement was too sensible of Michelangelo's merit to allow him to rust out his powers in petty tasks. He conceived the idea of erecting a chapel to be attached to the church of San Lorenzo, at Florence, to be the final resting-place of the great members of the Medici family. Michelangelo planned and built the chapel and for it wrought six great pieces of art. These are the statues of Lorenzo de Medici, father of Catherine de Medici (who was such a large, black blot on the page of history); a statue of Giuliano de Medici (whose name lives now principally because Michelangelo made this statue); and the four colossal reclining figures known as "Night," "Morning," "Dawn" and "Twilight." This chapel is now open to the public, and no visitor at Florence should miss seeing it.

The statue of Lorenzo must ever rank as one of the world's masterpieces. The Italians call it "Il Pensiero." The sullen strength of the attitude gives one a vague ominous impulse to get away. Some one has said that it fulfils Milton's conception of Satan brooding over his plans for the ruin of mankind ❧ ❧

In Fifteen Hundred Twenty-seven, while Michelangelo was working on the chapel, Florence was attacked and sacked by the Constable de Bourbon. The Medici family was again expelled, and from the leisurely decoration of a church in honor of the gentle Christ, the artist was called upon to build barricades to protect his native city. His ingenuity as an engineer was as consummate as his exquisite idea of harmony, and for nine months the city was defended ❧

Through treachery the enemy was then allowed to enter and Michelangelo fled. Riots and wars seem as natural as thunderstorms to the Latin people; but after a year the clouds rolled by, Michelangelo was pardoned, and went back to his work of beautifying the chapel of San Lorenzo ❧ ❧

In Fifteen Hundred Thirty-four, Pope Clement was succeeded by Paul the Third. Paul was seventy years old, but the vigor of his mind was very much like that of the great Julius. His first desire was to complete the decoration of the Sistine Chapel, so that the entire interior should match the magnificence of the ceiling, and to the task he summoned Michelangelo ❧ ❧

# MICHELANGELO

The great artist hesitated. The ceiling was his supreme work as a painter, and he knew down deep in his heart that he could not hope to surpass it, and the risk of not equaling it was too great for him to run. The matter was too delicately personal to explain—only an artist could understand ✤ Michelangelo made excuses to the Pope and declared he had forgotten how to use a brush, that his eyesight was bad, and that the only thing he could do was to carve.

But Paul was not to be turned aside, and reluctantly Michelangelo went back to the Sistine, that he had left over twenty years before.

Then it was that he painted "The Last Judgment" on the wall of the upper end of the chapel. Hamerton calls this the grandest picture ever executed, at the same time acknowledging its faults in taste. But it must be explained that the design was the conception of Julius, endorsed by Pope Paul, and it surely mirrors the spiritual qualities (or lack of them) in these men better than any biography possibly could.

The merciful Redeemer is shown as a muscular athlete, full of anger and the spirit of revenge—proud, haughty, fierce. The condemned are ranged before him—a confused mass of naked figures, suspended in all attitudes of agony and terrible foreboding. The "saved" are ranged on one side, and do not seem to be of much better intellectual and spiritual quality than the damned; very naturally they are quite pleased to think that it is the others who are damned, and not they. The entire conception reveals that masterly ability to portray the human figure in every attitude of fear or passion. A hundred years after the picture was painted, some dignitary took it into his head that portions of the work were too "daring"; and a painter was set at work robing the figures. His fussy attempts are quite apparent.

¶ Michelangelo's next work was to decorate the Paolina Chapel. As in his last work on the Sistine, he was constantly interrupted and advised and criticized ✣ As he worked, cardinals, bishops and young artists watched and suggested, but still the "Conversion of Saint Paul" and the "Crucifixion of Saint Peter," in the Paolina, must ever rank as masterly art ✣ ✣

The frescoes in the Paolina Chapel occupied seven years and ended the great artist's career as a painter. He was seventy-three years old.

Pope Paul then made him Chief Architect of Saint Peter's. Michelangelo knew the difficulties to be encountered—the bickerings, jealousies and criticisms that were inseparable from the work—and was only moved to accept the place on Pope Paul's declaration that no one else could do as well, and that it was the will of God. Michelangelo looked upon it as a duty and accepted the task, refusing to take any recompense for his services. He continued to discharge the duties of the office under the direction of Popes Paul, Pius the Fourth and Pius the Fifth. In all he worked under the pontificates of seven different popes.

The dome of Saint Peter's, soaring to the skies, is his finest monument. The self-sustaining, airy quality in this stupendous structure hushes the beholder into silence; and yet that same quality of poise, strength and sufficiency marks all of the work of this colossus, whether it be painting, architecture or sculpture. America has paid tribute to Michelangelo's genius by reproducing the dome of Saint Peter's over the Capitol at Washington.

Michelangelo died in Rome, aged eighty-nine, working and planning to the last. His sturdy frame showed health in every part, and he ceased to breathe just as a clock runs down. His remains were secretly taken to Florence and buried in the church of Santa Croce. A fine bust marks the spot, but the visitor can not help feeling a regret that the dust of this marvelous man does not rest beneath the zenith of the dome of Saint Peter's at Rome.

SITTING calmly in this quiet corner, and with closed eyes, viewing Michelangelo's life as a whole, the impression is one of heroic strength, battling with fierce passions, and becoming victor over them by working them up into art. The mold of the man was masculine, and the subdued sorrow that flavors his whole career never degenerates into sickly sentimentality or repining.

The sonnets of Michelangelo, recently given to the world, were written when he was nearly seventy years old. Several of the sonnets are directly addressed to Vittoria Colonna, and no doubt she inspired the whole volume. A writer of the time has mentioned his accidentally finding Michelangelo and Vittoria Colonna seated side by side in the dim twilight of a deserted church, "talking soft and low." Deserted churches have ever been favorite trysting-places for lovers; and one is glad for this little glimpse of quiet and peace in the tossing, troubled life-journey of this tireless man. In fact, the few years of warm friendship with Vittoria Colonna is a charmed and temperate space, without which the struggle and unrest would be so ceaseless as to be appalling. Sweet, gentle and helpful was their mutual friendship. At this period of Michelangelo's life we know that the vehemence of his emotions subsided, and tranquillity and peace were his for the rest of his life, such as he had never known before.

¶ The woman who stepped out of high society and won the love of this stern yet gentle old man must have been of a mental and spiritual quality to command our highest praise. The world loves Vittoria Colonna because she loved Michelangelo, and led him away from strife and rivalry and toil.

**REMBRANDT**

BRANDT

# REMBRANDT

THE eyes and the mouth are the supremely significant features of the human face. In Rembrandt's portraits the eye is the center wherein life, in its infinity of aspect, is most manifest. Not only was his fidelity absolute, but there is a certain mysterious limpidity of gaze that reveals the soul of the sitter. A "Rembrandt" does not give up its beauties to the casual observer—it takes time to know it, but once known, it is yours forever.—Emile Michel.

# REMBRANDT

SWIMMING uneasily in my ink-bottle is a small preachment concerning names, and the way they have been evolved, and lost, or added to. Some day I will fish this effusion out and give it to a waiting world. Those of us whose ancestors landed at Plymouth or Jamestown are very proud of our family names, and even if we trace quite easily to Castle Garden we do not always discard the patronymic.

Harmen Gerritsz was a young man who lived in the city of Leyden, Holland, in the latter part of the Sixteenth Century. The letters "sz" at the end of his name stood for "szoon" and signified that he was the szoon of Mynheer Gerrit.

Now Harmen Gerritsz duly served an apprenticeship with a miller, and when his time expired, being of an ambitious nature, he rented a mill on the city wall, and started business for himself. Shortly after he very naturally married the daughter of a baker.

All of Mr. Harmen Gerritsz's customers called him Harmen, and when they wished to be exact they spoke of him as Harmen van Ryn—that is to say, Harmen of the Rhine, for his mill was near the river. "Out West," even now, if you call a man

Mister, he will probably inquire what it is you have against him ✦ ✦

Mr. and Mrs. Harmen lived in the mill, and as years went by were blessed with a nice little family of six children. The fifth child is the only one that especially interests us. They named him Rembrandt.

Rembrandt Harmenszoon van Ryn, he called himself when he entered at the grammar-school at Leyden, aged fourteen. His father's first name being Harmen, he simply took that, and discarded the Gerrit entirely, according to the custom of the time. In fact, all our Johnsons are the sons of John, and the names Peterson, Thompson and Wilson, in feudal times, had their due and proper significance. Then when we find names with a final ending of "s," such as Robbins, Larkins and Perkins, we are to understand that the owner is the son of his father. And so we find Rembrandt Harmenszoon in his later years writing his name Harmensz and then simply Harmens.

Mynheer Harmen Gerritszoon's windmill ground exceeding small, and the product found a ready market. There were no servants in the miller's family—everybody worked at the business. In Holland people are industrious. The leisurely ways of the Dutch can, I think, safely be ascribed to their environment, and here is an argument Buckle might have inserted in his great book, but did not, and so I will write it down.

There are windmills in Holland (I trust the fact need not longer be concealed) and these windmills are used for every possible mechanical purpose. Now the wind blows only a part of the time—excepting in Chicago—and there may be whole days when not a windmill turns in all Holland. The men go out in the morning and take due note of the wind, and if there is an absolute calm many of them go back to bed. I have known the wind to die down during the day and the whole force of a windmill troop off to a picnic, as a matter of course. So the elements in Holland set man the example—he will not rush himself to death when not even the wind does.

Then another thing: Holland has many canals. Farmers load their hay on canal-boats and take it to the barn, women go to market in boats, lovers sail, seemingly, right across the fields—canals everywhere.

Traveling by canal is not rapid transit. So the people of Holland have plenty of precedent for moving at a moderate speed. There are no mountains in Holland, so water never runs; it may move, but the law of gravitation there only acts to keep things quiet. The Dutch never run footraces —neither do they scorch.

In Amsterdam I have seen a man sit still for an hour, and this with a glass of beer before him, gazing off into space, not once winking, not even thinking. You can not do that in America where trolley-cars whiz and blizzards blow—there is no precedent for it in things animate or inanimate. In the United States everything is on the jump, art included.

Rembrandt Harmens worked in his father's mill, but never strained his back. He was healthy, needlessly healthy, and was as smart as his brothers and sisters, but no smarter, and no better looking. He was exceedingly self-contained, and would sit and dream at his desk in the grammar-school, looking out straight in front of him—just at nothing.

The master tried flogging, and the next day found a picture of himself on the blackboard, his face portrayed as anything but lovely. Young Rembrandt was sent home to fetch his father. The father came.

"Look at that!" said the irate teacher; "see what your son did; look at that!"

Mynheer Harmen sat down and looked at the picture in his deliberate Dutch way, and after about fifteen minutes said, "Well, it does look like you!"

Then he explained to the schoolmaster that the lad was sent to school because he would not do much around the mill but draw pictures in the dust, and it was hoped that the schoolmaster could teach him something.

The schoolmaster decided that it was a hopeless case, and the miller went home to report to the boy's mother.

Now whenever a Dutchman is confronted by a problem too big to solve, or a task too unpleasant for him to undertake, he shows his good sense by turning it over to his wife.

"You are his mother, anyway," said Harmen van Ryn, reproachfully ❧ ❧

The mother simply waived the taunt and asked, "Do you tell me the schoolmaster says he will not do anything but draw pictures?"

"Not a tap will he do but make pictures—he can not multiply two by one."

"Well," said the mother, "if he will not do anything but draw pictures, I think we 'd better let him draw pictures."

**A**T that early age I do not think Rembrandt was ambitious to be a painter. Good healthy boys of fourteen are not hampered and harassed by ambition—ambition, like love, camps hot upon our trail later. Ambition is the concomitant of rivalry, and sex is its chief promoter—it is a secondary sex manifestation.

The boy simply had a little intuitive skill in drawing, and the exercise of the talent was a gratification. It pleased him to see the semblance of face or form unfold before him. It was a kind of play, a working off of surplus energy.

Had the lad's mind at that time been forcibly diverted to books or business, it is very probable that today the catalogs would be without the name of Rembrandt.

But mothers have ambitions, even if boys have not—they wish to see their children do things that other women's children can not do. Among wild animals the mother kills, when she can, all offspring but her own. Darwin refers to mother-love as, "that instinct in the mind of the female which causes her to exaggerate the importance of her offspring—often protecting them to the death." Through this instinct of protection is the species preserved. In human beings mother-love is well flavored with pride, prejudice, jealousy and ambition ☙ This is because the mother is a woman. And this is well—God made it all, and did He not look upon His work and pronounce it good?

The mother of Rembrandt knew that in Leyden there were men who painted beautiful pictures. She had seen these pictures at the University, and in the Town Hall and in the churches; and she had overheard men discussing and criticizing the work. She herself was poor and uneducated, her husband was only a miller, with no recreation beyond the beer-garden and a clicking reluctantly off to church in his wooden shoes on Sunday. They had no influential friends, no learned patrons—the men at the University never so much as nodded to millers. Her lot was lowly, mean, obscure, and filled with drudgery and pettiness. And now some one was saying her boy Rembrandt was lazy; he would neither work nor study. The taunt stung her mother-pride—"He will do nothing but make pictures!"

Ah! a great throb came to her heart. Her face flushed, she saw it all—all in prophetic vision stood out like an etching on the blankness of the future. "He will do nothing but draw pictures? Very well then, he shall draw pictures! He will draw so well that they shall adorn the churches of Leyden, and the Town Hall, and yes! even the churches of Amsterdam. Holland shall be proud of my boy! He will teach other men to draw, his pictures will command fabulous prices, and his name shall be honored everywhere! Yes, my boy shall draw pictures! This day will I take him to Mynheer Jacob van Swanenburch, who was a pupil of the great Rubens, and who has scholars even from Antwerpen. I will take him to the Master, and I will say, 'Mynheer, I am only a poor woman, the daughter of an honest baker. My husband is a miller. This is my son. He will do nothing but draw pictures. Here is a bag of gold—not much, but it is all good gold; there are no bad coins in this bag; I've been ten years in saving them. Take this bag—it is yours —now teach my son to paint. Teach him as you taught

Valderschoon and those others—my memory is bad, I can not remember the names—I'm only a poor woman. Show my boy how to paint. And when I am dead, and you are dead, men will come to your grave and say, "It is here that he rests, here—the man who first taught Rembrandt Harmenszoon to use a brush!" Do you hear, Mynheer Van Swanenburch? The gold—it is yours—and this is my boy!'"

**J**ACOB VAN SWANENBURCH belonged to one of the aristocratic families of Leyden. His father had been burgomaster, and he himself occupied from time to time offices of importance. He was not a great painter, although several specimens of his work still adorn the Town Hall of his native city.

Rembrandt was not very anxious to attend Swanenburch's classes. He was a hesitating, awkward youth and on this account was regarded as unsocial. For a year the boy looked on, listened, and made straight marks and curves and all that. He did not read and the world of art was a thing unknown to him.

There are two kinds of people to be found in all studios: those who talk about art, and the fellows who paint the pictures ✌ ✌

However, Rembrandt was an exception, and for a time would do neither. He would not paint, because he said he could not—anyway he would not; but no doubt he did a deal of thinking. This habit of reticence kept him in the background, and even the master had suspicions that he was too beefy to hold a clear mental conception.

The error of the Swanenburch atelier lay in the fact that quiet folks are not necessarily stupid. It is doubtless true, however, that stupid men by remaining quiet may often pass for men of wisdom: this is because no man can really talk as wisely as he can look.

Young Rembrandt was handicapped by a full-moon face, and small gray eyes that gave no glint, and his hair was so towsled and unruly that he could not wear a hat.

So the sons of aristocrats who cracked sly jokes at the miller's boy had their fun.

Rembrandt usually came in late, after the master had begun his little morning lecture. The lad was barefoot, having left his wooden shoon in the hallway "so as not to wear out the floor." He would bow awkwardly to the professor, fall over a chair or two that had been slyly pushed in his way, and taking his seat chew the butt end of a brush.

"Why are you always late?" asked the master one day.

"Oh, I was working at home and forgot the time."

"And what are you working at?"

"Me? I'm—I'm drawing a little," and he colored vermilion to the back of his neck.

"Well, bring your work here so we can profit by it," exclaimed a joker, and the class guffawed.

The next morning the lad brought his picture—a woman's face—a picture of a face, homely, wrinkled, weather-beaten, but with a look of love and patience and loyalty beaming out of the quiet eyes.

"Who did this?" demanded the teacher.

Rembrandt hesitated, stuttered, stammered, and then confessed that he did it himself—he could not tell a lie.

He was sure the picture would be criticized and ridiculed, but he had decided to face it out. It was a picture of his mother, and he had sketched her just as she looked. He would let them laugh, and then at noon he would wait outside the door and smash the boy who laughed loudest over the head with a wooden shoe—and let it go at that.

But the scholars did not laugh, for Jacob van Swanenburch

took the boy by the hand and leading him out before the class told those young men to look upon their master.

From that time forth Rembrandt was regarded by the little art world of Leyden as a prodigy.

Like William Cullen Bryant, who wrote "Thanatopsis" when scarcely eighteen, and writing for sixty years thereafter never equaled it, or Dante Gabriel Rossetti, who wrote "The Blessed Damozel" at the same age, Rembrandt sprang into life full armed.

It is probably true that he could not then have produced an elaborate composition, but his faces were Rembrandtesque from the very first.

Rembrandt is the king of light and shade. You never mistake his work. As the years passed, around him clustered a goodly company of pupils, hundreds in all, who diligently worked to catch the trick, but Rembrandt stands alone. "He is the only artist who could ever paint a wrinkle," says Ruskin. All his portraits have the warts on. And the thought has often come to me that only a Rembrandt—the only Rembrandt—could have portrayed the face of Lincoln. Plain, homely, awkward, eyes not mates, sunken cheeks, leathery skin, moles, uncombed hair, neckcloth askew; but over and above and beyond all a look of power—and the soul! that look of haunting sorrow and the great, gentle soul within!

¶ And so there is a picture of Rembrandt's mother which this son painted that must ever stand out as one of the world's masterpieces.

Let who will, declare that the portrait by Richter in the Gallery at Cologne, of Queen Louise, is the handsomest portrait ever painted; yet the depth of feeling, the dignity and love in the homely old mother's face, pale not in comparison, but are things to which the proud and beautiful Queen herself paid homage.

Rembrandt painted nearly a hundred pictures of his mother that we can trace. In most of them she holds in her hands a little Bible, and thus did the son pay tribute to her devoted piety. She was a model of which he never tired. He painted her in court dress, and various other fantastic garbs, that she surely never wore. He painted her as a nun, as a queen, a court beauty, a plain peasant, a musician; and in various large pictures her face and form are introduced. And most of these pictures of his mother are plainly signed with his monogram. He also painted his sister as the Madonna, and this is signed; but although he doubtless painted his father's face, yet he did not sign such pictures, so their authenticity is a hazard. This fact gives a clue to his affections which each can work out for himself.

Rembrandt remained with Swanenburch for three years, and the master proved his faithful friend. He gave him an introduction into the aristocratic art world which otherwise might have barred its doors against so profound a genius, as aristocracy has done time and again.

The best artists are not necessarily the best teachers. If a man has too much skill along a certain line he will overpower and kill the individuality in his pupil ✤ There are teachers who smother a pupil with their own personality, and thus it often happens that the strongest men are not the most useful as instructors. The ideal teacher is not the one who bends all minds to match his own; but the one who is able to bring out and develop the good that is in the pupil—him we will crown with laurel.

Swanenburch was pretty nearly the ideal teacher. His good nature, the feminine quality of sympathy in his character, his freedom from all petty, quibbling prejudice, and his sublime patience all worked to burst the tough husk, and develop that shy and sensitive, yet uncouth and silent youth, bringing out the best that was in him. A wrong environment in those early years might easily have shaped Rembrandt into a morose and resentful dullard: the good in his nature, thrown back upon itself, would have been turned to gall.

THE little business on the city wall had prospered, and Harmen van Ryn moved, with his family, out of the old mill into a goodly residence across the street. He was carrying his head higher, and the fact that his son Rembrandt was being invited to the homes of the professors at the University was incidentally thrown off, until the patrons at the beer-garden grew aweary and rapped their glasses on the table as a signal for silence.

Swanenburch had given a public exhibition of the work of his pupils, at which young Rembrandt had been pushed forward as an example of what right methods in pedagogics could do.

"Well, why can not all your scholars draw like that, then?" asked a broad-beamed Dutchman.

"They certainly could, if they would follow the principles I lay down," answered the master severely.

But admiration did not spoil Rembrandt. His temperature was too low for ebullition—he took it all quite as a matter of course. His work was done with such ease that he was not aware it was extraordinary in quality; and when Swanenburch sold several of his sketches at goodly prices and put the silver in the lad's hand, he asked who the blockheads were who had invested.

Swanenburch taught his pupils the miracle of spreading a thin coat of wax on a brass plate, and drawing a picture in the wax with a sharp graver; then acid was poured over it and the acid ate into the brass so as to make a plate from which you could print. Etching was a delight to Rembrandt. Expert illustrators of books were in demand at Leyden, for it was then the bookmaking center of Northern Europe. The Elzevirs were pushing the Plantins of Antwerp hard for first place.

So skilfully did Rembrandt sketch, that one of the great printers made a proposition to his father to take the boy until he was twenty-one, and pay the father a thousand florins a year for the lad's services as an illustrator. The father accepted the proposition; and the next day brought around another Harmenszoon that he declared was just as good. But the bookmaker was stubborn and insisted on having a certain one or none. So the bargain fell through.

¶ It was getting near four years since Swanenburch had taken Rembrandt into his keeping, and now he went to the boy's parents and said: "I have given all I have to offer to your son. He can do all I can, and more. There is only one man who can benefit him and that is Pieter Lastman, of Amsterdam. He must go and study with the great Lastman—I myself will take him."

Lastman had spent four years in Italy, and had come back full to overflowing with classic ideas. His family was one of the most aristocratic in Amsterdam, and whatever he said concerning art was quoted as final. He was the court of last appeal. His rooms were filled with classic fragments, and on his public days visitors flocked to hear what he might have to say about the wonders of Venice, Florence and Rome. For in those days men seldom traveled out of their own countries, and those who did had strange tales to tell the eager listeners when they returned.

Lastman was handsome, dashing, popular. His pictures

were in demand, principally because they were Lastman's. Proud ladies came from afar and begged the privilege of sitting as his model. In Italy, Lastman had found that many painters employed 'prentice talent. The great man would sketch out the pictures, and the boys would fill in the color. Lastman would go off about his business, and perhaps drop in occasionally during the day to see how the boys got on, adding a few touches here and there, and gently rebuking those who showed too much genius. Lastman believed in genius, of course; but only his own genius filled his ideal. As a consequence, all of Lastman's pictures are alike—they are all equally bad. They represent neither the Italian school nor the Dutch, being hybrids: Italian skies and Holland backgrounds; Dutchmen dressed as dagoes.

Lastman was putting money in his purse. He closely studied public tastes, and conformed thereto. He was popular, and there is in America today a countryman of his, of like temperament, who is making much monies out of literature by similar methods.

Into Lastman's keeping came the young man, Rembrandt Harmens. Lastman received him cordially, and set him to work ♣ ♣

But the boy proved hard to manage: he had his own ideas about how portraits should be painted.

Lastman tried to unlearn him. The master was patient, and endeavored hard to make the young man paint as he should—that is, as Lastman did; but the result was not a success. The Lastman intellect felt sure that Rembrandt had no talent worth encouraging.

Lastman produced a great number of pictures, and his name can be found in the catalogs of the galleries of Amsterdam, Munich, Berlin and Antwerp; and his canvases are in many of the old castles and palaces of Germany. In recent years they have been enjoying a vogue, simply because it was possible that Rembrandt had worked on them ❧ All the "Lastmans" have been gotten out and thoroughly dusted by the connoisseurs, in a frantic search for earmarks.

The perfect willingness of Lastman to paint a picture on any desired subject, and have it ready Saturday night, all in the colors the patron desired, with a guarantee that it would give satisfaction, filled the heart of Rembrandt with loathing ❧ ❧

At the end of six months, when he signified a wish to leave, it was a glad relief to the master. Lastman had tried to correct Rembrandt's vagaries as to chiaroscuro, but without success. So he wrote an ambiguous letter certifying to the pupil's "having all his future before him," gave him a present of ten florins in jingling silver, and sent him back to his folks.

Rembrandt had been disillusioned by his stay in the fashionable art-world of Amsterdam. Some of his idols had crumbled, and there came into his spirit a goodly dash of pessimism. His father was disappointed and suggested that he get a place as illustrator at the book-makers, before some one else stepped in and got the job ✤ But Rembrandt was not ambitious. He decided he would not give up painting, at least not yet—he would keep at it and he would paint as he pleased. He had lost faith in teachers. He moped around the town, and made the acquaintance of the painter Engelbrechtsz and his talented pupil, Lucas van Leyden. Their work impressed him greatly, and he studied out every detail on the canvases until he had absorbed the very spirit of the artist. Then, when he painted, he very naturally took their designs, and treated them in his own way. Indeed, the paucity in invention of those early days must ever impress the student of art.

In visiting the galleries of Europe, I made it my business to secure a photograph of every "Madonna and Babe" of note that I could find. My collection now numbers over one hundred copies, with no two alike.

The Madonna, of course, is the extreme example; but there are dozens of "The Last Supper," "Abraham's Sacrifice," "The Final Judgment," "The Brazen Serpent," "Raising of Lazarus," "The Annunciation," "Rebekah at the Well" and so on.

If one painter produced a notable picture, all the other artists in the vicinity felt it their duty to treat the same subject; in fact, their honor was at stake—they just had to, in order to satisfy the clamor of their friends, and meet the challenges of detractors.

This "progressive sketching" was kept up, each man improving, or trying to improve, on the attempts of the former, until a Leonardo struck twelve and painted his "Last Supper," or a Rubens did his "Descent From the Cross"—then competitors grew pale, and tried their talent on a lesser theme.

One of the most curious examples of the tendency to follow a bellwether is found in the various pictures called "The Anatomy Lesson." When Venice was at its height, in the year Fourteen Hundred Ninety-two—a date we can easily remember—an unknown individual drew a picture of a professor of anatomy; on a table in the center is a naked human corpse, while all around are ranged the great doctor's pupils. Dissection had just been introduced into Venice at that time, and in a treatise on the subject by Andrea Vesali, I find that it became quite the fad. The lecture-rooms were open to the public, and places were set apart for women visitors and the nobility, while all around the back were benches for the plain people. On the walls were skeletons, and in cases were arranged saws, scalpels, needles, sponges and various other implements connected with the cheerful art ❧ ❧

The Unknown's picture of this scene made a sensation. And straightway other painters tried their hands at it, the unclothed form of the corpse affording a fine opportunity for the "classic touch." Paul Veronese tried it, and so did the Bellinis—Titian also.

Then a century passed, as centuries do, and the glory of Venice drifted to Amsterdam—commercially and artistically. Amsterdam painters used every design that the Venetians had, and some of their efforts were sorry attempts ✄ In Sixteen Hundred Twenty, following Venetian precedent, dissection became a fad in Leyden and Amsterdam. Swanenburch engraved a picture of the Leyden dissecting-room, with a brace of gallant doctors showing some fair ladies the beauties of the place. The Dutch were ambitious—the young men, Rembrandt included, drew pictures entitled, "The Lesson in Anatomy." Doctors who were getting on in the world gave orders for portraits, showing themselves as about to begin work on a subject. One physician, with intent to get even with his rival, had the artist picture the rival in the background as a pupil. Then the rival ordered a picture of himself, proud and beautiful, giving a lesson in anatomy, armed and equipped for business, and the cadaver was—the other doctor.

At the Chicago Fair, in Eighteen Hundred Ninety-three, there was shown a most striking "Anatomy Lesson" from the brush of a young New York artist. It pictures the professor removing the sheet from the face of the corpse, and we behold the features of a beautiful young woman.

Some day I intend to write a book entitled, "The Evolution and Possibilities of the Anatomy Lesson." Keep your eye on the subject—we are not yet through with it.

Swanenburch offered to give Rembrandt a room in his own house, but he preferred the old mill, and a wheat-bin was fitted up for a private studio. The fittings of the studio must have cost fully two dollars, according to all accounts; there were a three-legged stool, an easel, a wooden chest, and a straw bed in the corner. Only one window admitted the light, and this was so high up that the occupant was not troubled by visitors looking in.

Our best discoveries are the result of accident.

This single window, eight feet from the ground, allowed the rays of light to enter in a stream. On cloudy days and early in the mornings or in the evenings, Rembrandt noted that when the light fell on the face of the visitor the rest of the body was wholly lost in the shadow. He placed a curtain over the window with a varying aperture cut in it, and with his mother as model made numerous experiments in the effects of light and shade.

He seems to have been the very first artist who could draw a part of the form, leaving all the rest in absolute blackness, and yet give the impression to the casual onlooker that he sees the figure complete. Plain people with no interest in the technique of art will look upon a "Rembrandt," and go away and describe things in the picture that are not there. They will declare to you that they saw them—those obvious things which one fills in at once with his inward eye. For instance, there is a portrait of a soldier, by Rembrandt, in the Louvre, and above the soldier's head you see a tall cockade. You assume at once that this cockade is in the soldier's hat, but no hat is shown—not the semblance nor the outline of a hat. There is a slight line that might be the rim of a hat, or it might not. But not one person out of a thousand, looking upon the picture, but would go away and describe the hat, and be affronted if you should tell them there is no hat in the picture. Given a cockade, we assume a hat ✿ ✿

By the use of shadows Rembrandt threw the faces into relief; he showed the things he wished to show and emphasized one thing by leaving all else out. The success of art depends upon what you omit from your canvas. This masterly effect of illusion made the son of the miller stand out in the Leyden art-world like one of his own etchings.

Curiously enough, the effect of a new model made Rembrandt lose his cunning; with strangers he was self-conscious and ill at ease. His mother was his most patient model; his father and sisters took their turn; and then there was another model who stood Rembrandt in good stead. And that was himself. We have all seen children stand before a mirror and make faces. Rembrandt very early contracted this habit, and it evidently clung to him through life. He has painted his own portrait with expressions of hate, fear, pride, mirth, indifference, hope and wrath shown on his plastic features.

¶ There is also an old man with full white beard and white hair that Rembrandt has pictured again and again. This old man poses for "Lot," "Abraham," "Moses," "A Beggar," "A King," and once he even figures as "The Almighty." Who he was we do not know, and surely he did not realize the honor done him, or he would have written a proud word of explanation to be carved on his tomb.

IN the Stuttgart Museum is a picture entitled "Saint Paul in Prison," signed by Rembrandt, with the date Sixteen Hundred Twenty-seven. "The Money-Changers" in the Berlin Gallery bears the same signature and date. Rembrandt was then twenty years of age, and we see that he was doing good work. We also know that there was a certain market for his wares.

When twenty-two years of age his marvelous effects of light and shade attracted people who were anxious to learn how to do it. According to report he had sixteen pupils in Sixteen Hundred Twenty-eight, each of whom paid him the fixed sum of one hundred florins. This was not much, but it gave him an income equal to that of his father, and tended to confirm his faith in his own powers.

His energy was a surprise to all who had known him, for besides teaching his classes he painted, sketched and etched. Most of his etchings were of his own face—not intended as portraits, for they are often purposely disguised. It seemed to be the intent of the artist to run the whole gamut of the passions, portraying them on the human face. Six different etchings done in the year Sixteen Hundred Twenty-eight are to be seen in the British Museum.

His most intimate friend at this time was Jan Lievens. The bond that united them was a mutual contempt for Lastman of Amsterdam. In fact, they organized a club, the single qualification required of each candidate for admittance being a hatred for Lastman. This club met weekly at a beer-hall, and each member had to relate an incident derogatory to the Lastman school. At the close of each story, all solemnly drank eternal perdition to Lastman and his ilk. Finally, Lastman was invited to join; and in reply he wrote a gracious letter of acceptance. This surely shows that Lastman was pretty good quality, after all.

Rembrandt was making money. His pupils spread his praise, and so many new ones came that he took the old quarters of Swanenburch.

In Sixteen Hundred Thirty-one, there came to him a young man who was to build a deathless name for himself—Gerard Dou. Then to complete the circle came Joris van Vliet, whose reputation as an engraver must ever take a first rank. Van Vliet engraved many of Rembrandt's pictures, and did it so faithfully and with such loving care that copies today command fabulous prices among the collectors. Indeed, we owe to Van Vliet a debt for preserving many of Rembrandt's pictures, the originals of which have disappeared. With the help of Van Vliet the Elzevirs accomplished their wishes, and so made use of the talent of Rembrandt.

Rembrandt lived among the poor, as a matter of artistic policy, mingling with them on an absolute equality. He considered their attitudes simpler, more natural, and their conduct less artificial, than the manners of those in higher walks ⁂

About Sixteen Hundred Twenty-nine, there came into his hands a set of Callot's engravings, and the work produced on his mind a profound impression. Callot's specialty was beggardom. He pictured decrepit beggars, young beggars, handsome girl-beggars, and gallant old beggars who wore their fluttering rags with easy grace.

The man who could give the phlegmatic Rembrandt a list to starboard must have carried considerable ballast. Straightway on making Callot's acquaintance he went forth with bags of coppers and made the acquaintance of beggars. He did not have to travel far—"the Greeks were at his door." The news spread, and each morning, the truthful Orles has told us, "there were over four hundred beggars blocking the street that led to his study," all willing to enlist in the cause of art. For six months Rembrandt painted little beside "the ragged gentry." But he gradually settled down on about ten separate and distinct types of abject picturesqueness ✦ Ten years later, when he pictured the "Healing Christ," he introduced the Leyden beggars, and these fixed types that he carried hidden in the cells of his brain he introduced again and again in various pictures. In this respect he was like all good illustrators: he had his properties, and by new combinations made new pictures. Who has not noticed that every painter carries in his kit his own distinct types—sealed, certified to, and copyrighted by popular favor as his own personal property?

Can you mistake Kemble's "coons," Denslow's dandies, Remington's horses, Giannini's Indians, or Gibson's "Summer Girl"? These men may not be Rembrandts, but when we view the zigzag course art has taken, who dare prophesy that this man's name is writ in water and that man's carved in the granite of a mountain-side! Contemporary judgments usually have been wrong. Did the chief citizens of Leyden in the year Sixteen Hundred Thirty regard Rembrandt's beggars as immortal? Not exactly!

# REMBRANDT

IN Sixteen Hundred Thirty-one, Rembrandt concluded that his reputation in the art-world of Holland was sufficient for him to go to Amsterdam and boldly pit himself against De Keyser, Hals, Lastman and the rest. He had put forth his "Lesson in Anatomy," and the critics and connoisseurs who had come from the metropolis to see it were lavish in their praise. Later we find him painting the subject again with another doctor handling the tweezers and scalpel.

Rembrandt started for Amsterdam the second time—this time as a teacher, not as a scholar. He rented an old warehouse on the canal for a studio. It was nearly as outlandish a place as his former quarters in the mill at Leyden. But it gave him plenty of room, was secluded, and afforded good opportunity for experiments in light and shade.

He seemed to have gotten over his nervousness in working with strange models; for new faces now begin to appear. One of these is that of a woman, and it would have been well for his art had he never met her. We see her face quite often, and in the "Diana Bathing" we behold her altogether ✄ Rembrandt shows small trace of the classic instinct, for classic art is founded on poetic imagination. Rembrandt painted what he saw, the Greeks portrayed that which they felt; and when Rembrandt paints a Dutch wench and calls her "Diana," he unconsciously illustrates the difference between the naked and the nude. Rembrandt painted this same woman, wearing no clothes to speak of, lolling on a couch; and evidently considering the subject a little risky, thought to give it dignity by a Biblical title: "Potiphar's

Wife." One good look at this picture, and the precipitate flight of Joseph is fully understood. We feel like following his example.

Rembrandt had simply haunted the dissecting-rooms of the University at Leyden a little too long.

The study of these viragos scales down our rating of the master. Still, I suppose every artist has to go through this period—the period when he thinks he is called upon to portray the feminine form divine—it is like the mumps and the measles.

After a year of groping for he knew not what, with money gone, and not much progress made, Rembrandt took a reef in his pride and settled down to paint portraits, and to do a little good honest teaching.

Scholars came to him, and commissions for portraits began to arrive. He renounced the freaks of costume, illumination and attitude, and painted the customer in plain, simple, Dutch dress. He let "Diana" go, and went soberly to work to make his fortune.

Holland was prosperous. Her ships sailed every sea, and brought rich treasures home. The prosperous can afford to be generous. Philanthropy became the fad. Charity was in the air, and hospitals, orphanages and homes for the aged were established. The rich merchants felt it an honor to serve on the board of managers of these institutions ✣ In each of the guildhalls were parlors set apart for deliberative gatherings; and it became the fashion to embellish these rooms with portraits of the managers, trustees and donors ✣ ✣

Rembrandt's portraits were finding their way to the guilds. They attracted much attention, and orders came—orders for more work than the artist could do. He doubled his prices in the hope of discouraging applicants.

Studio gossip and society chatter seemed to pall on young Rembrandt. It is said that when a 'bus-driver has a holiday he always goes and rides with the man who is taking his place; but when Rembrandt had a holiday he went away from the studio, not towards it. He would walk alone, off across the meadows, and along the canals, and once we find him tramping off thirty miles to visit cousins who were fishermen on the seacoast. Happy fisher-folk!

But Rembrandt took few play-spells; he broke off entirely from his tavern companions and lived the life of an ascetic and recluse, seeing no society except the society that came to his studio. His heart was in his art, and he was intent on working while it was called the day.

About this time there came to him Cornelis Sylvius, the eminent preacher, to sit for a picture that was to adorn the Seaman's Orphanage, of which Sylvius was director. It took a good many sittings to bring out a Rembrandt portrait. On one of his visits the clergyman was accompanied by a young woman—his ward—by name, Saskia van Ulenburgh ♣ ♣

The girl was bright, animated and intelligent, and as she sat in the corner the painter sort of divided his attention between her and the clergyman. Then the girl got up, walked about a bit, looking at the studio properties, and finally stood behind the young painter, watching him work. This was one of the things Rembrandt could never, never endure ❧ It paralyzed his hand, and threw all his ideas into a jumble. It was the law of his studio that no one should watch him paint—he had secrets of technique that had cost him great labor ❧ ❧

"You do not mind my watching you work?" asked the ingenuous girl.

"Oh, not in the least!"

"You are quite sure my presence will not make you nervous, then?"

Rembrandt said something to the effect that he rather liked to have some one watch him when he worked; it depended, of course, on who it was—and asked the sitter to elevate his chin a little and not look so cross.

Next day Saskia came again to watch the transfer of the good uncle's features to canvas.

The young artist was first among the portrait-painters of Amsterdam, and had a long waiting-list on his calendar, but we find he managed to paint a portrait of Saskia about that time. We have the picture now and we also have four or five other pictures of her that Rembrandt produced that year. He painted her as a queen, as a court lady and as a flower-girl. The features may be disguised a little, but it is the same fine, bright, charming, petite young woman ❧

Before six months had passed he painted several more portraits of Saskia; and in one of these she has a sprig of rosemary—the emblem of betrothal—held against her heart ❧ ❧

And then we find an entry at the Register's to the effect

that they were married on June Twenty-fourth, Sixteen Hundred Thirty-four.

Rembrandt's was a masterly nature: strong, original and unyielding. But the young woman had no wish that was not his, and her one desire was to make her lover happy. She was not a great woman, but she was good, which is better, and she filled her husband's heart to the brim. Those first few years of their married life read like a fairy-tale ✤ He bought her jewels, laces, elegant costumes, and began to fill their charming home with many rare objects of art. All was for Saskia—his life, his fortune, his work, his all.
¶ As the years go by we shall see that it would have been better had he saved his money and builded against the coming of the storm; but even though Saskia protested mildly against his extravagance, the master would have his way ✤ ✤

His was a tireless nature: he found his rest in change. He usually had some large compositions on hand and turned to this for pastime when portraits failed. Then Saskia was ever present, and if there was a holiday he painted her as the "Jewish Bride," "The Gypsy Queen," or in some other fantastic garb.

We have seen that in those early years at Leyden he painted himself, but now it was only Saskia—she was his other self. All those numerous pictures of himself were drawn before he knew Saskia—or after she had gone.

Their paradise continued nine years—and then Saskia died.
¶ Rembrandt was not yet forty when desolation settled down upon him ✤ ✤

ASKIA was the mother of five children; four of them had died, and the babe she left, Titus by name, was only eight months old when she passed away.

For six months we find that Rembrandt did very little. He was stunned, and his brain and hand refused to co-operate.

¶ The first commission he undertook was the portrait of the wife of one of the rich merchants of the city. When the work was done, the picture resembled the dead Saskia so much more than it did the sitter that the patron refused to accept it. The artist saw only Saskia and continued to portray her.

¶ But work gave him rest, and he began a series of Biblical studies—serious, sober scenes fitted to his mood. His hand had not lost its cunning, for there is a sureness and individuality shown in his work during the next few years that stamps him as the Master.

But his rivals raised a great clamor against his style. They declared that he trampled on all precedent and scorned the laws on which true art is built. However, he had friends, and they, to help him, went forth and secured the commission —the famous "Night-Watch," now in the Ryks Museum at Amsterdam.

The production of this fine picture resulted in a comedy of errors, that shaded off into a tragedy for poor Rembrandt. The original commission for this picture came from thirty-seven prominent citizens, who were to share the expense equally between them. The order was for the portraits of the eminent men to appear on one canvas, the subjects to be grouped in an artistic way according to the artist's own conceit ✣ ✣

# REMBRANDT

Rembrandt studied hard over the matter, as he was not content to execute a picture of a mass of men doing nothing but pose.

It took a year to complete the picture. The canvas shows a band of armed men, marching forth to the defense of the city in response to a sudden night alarm. Two brave men lead the throng and the others shade off into mere Rembrandt shadows, and you only know there are men there by the nodding plumes, banners and spearheads that glisten in the pale light of the torches.

When the picture was unveiled, the rich donors looked for themselves on the canvas, and some looked in vain. Only two men were satisfied, and these were the two who marched in the vanguard.

"Where am I?" demanded a wealthy shipowner of Rembrandt as the canvas was scanned in a vain search for his proud features.

"You see the palace there in the picture, do you not?" asked the artist petulantly.

"Yes, I see that," was the answer.

' Well, you are behind that palace."

The company turned on Rembrandt, and forbade the hanging of any more of his pictures in the municipal buildings.

Rembrandt shrugged his shoulders. But as the year passed and orders dropped away, he found how unwise a thing it is to affront the public. Men who owed him refused to pay, and those whom he owed demanded their money.

He continued doggedly on his course.

Some years before he had bought a large house and borrowed

money to pay for it, and had further given his note at hand to various merchants and dealers in curios. As long as he was making money no one cared for more than the interest, but now the principal was demanded. So sure had Rembrandt been of his powers that he did not conceive that his income could drop from thirty thousand florins a year to scarcely a fifth of that.

Then his relations with Hendrickje Stoffels had displeased society. She was his housekeeper, servant and model—a woman without education or refinement, we are told. But she was loyal, more than loyal, to Rembrandt: she lived but to serve him and sought to protect his interests in every way. When summoned before the elders of the church to answer for her conduct, she appeared, pleaded guilty and shocked the company by declaring, "I would rather go to Hell with Rembrandt Harmens than play a harp in Heaven, surrounded by such as you!"

The remark was bruited throughout the city and did Rembrandt no good. His rivals combined to shut his work out of all exhibitions, and several made it their business to buy up the overdue claims against him.

Then officers came and took possession of his house, and all his splendid collection of jewels, laces, furniture, curios and pictures were sold at auction. The fine dresses that once belonged to Saskia were seized: they even took her wedding-gown: and wanton women bid against the nobility for the possession of these things. Rembrandt was stripped of his sketches, and these were sold in bundles—the very sweat of his brain for years. Then he was turned into the streets

But Hendrickje Stoffels still clung to him, his only friend. Rembrandt's proud heart was broken. He found companionship at the taverns; and to get a needful loaf of bread for Hendrickje and his boy, made sketches and hawked them from house to house.

Fashions change and art is often only a whim ✿ People wondered why they had ever bought those dark, shadowy things made by that Leyden artist, What's-his-name! One man utilized the frames which contained "Rembrandts" by putting other canvases right over in front of them.

Rembrandt's son Titus tried his skill at art, but with indifferent success. He died while yet a youth. Then Hendrickje passed away, and Rembrandt was alone—a battered derelict on the sea of life. He lost his identity under an assumed name, and sketched with chalk on tavern-walls and pavement for the amusement of the crowd.

He died in Sixteen Hundred Sixty-nine, and the expense of his burial was paid by the hands of charity.

The cost of the funeral was seven dollars and fifty cents ✿

---

In Eighteen Hundred Ninety-seven, there was sold in London a small portrait by Rembrandt for a sum equal to a trifle more than thirty-one thousand dollars. But even this does not represent the true value of one of his pictures—for connoisseurs regard a painting by Rembrandt as priceless.

There is a law in Holland forbidding any one on serious penalty to remove a "Rembrandt" from the country. If any one of the men who combined to work his ruin is mentioned in history, it is only to say, "He lived in the age of Rembrandt."

RUBENS

# RUBENS

I WAS admitted to the Duke of Lerma's presence, and took part in the embassy. The Duke exhibited great satisfaction at the excellence and number of the pictures, which surely have acquired a certain fair appearance of antiquity (by means of my retouching), in spite even of the damage they had undergone. They are held and accepted by the King and Queen as originals, without there being any doubt on their side, or assertion on ours, to make them believe them to be such.—Letter from Rubens at Madrid, to Chieppo, Secretary of the Duke of Mantua.

# RUBENS

THE father of Peter Paul Rubens was a lawyer, a man of varied attainments and marked personality. In statecraft he showed much skill, and by his ability in business management served William the Silent, Prince of Orange, in good stead.

But Jan Rubens had a bad habit of thinking for himself. The habit grew upon him until the whisper was passed from this one to that, that he was becoming decidedly atheistic.

Spain held a strong hand upon Antwerp, and the policy of Philip the Second was to crush opposition in the bud. Jan Rubens had criticized Spanish rule, and given it as his opinion that the Latin race would not always push its domination upon the people of the North.

At this time Spain was so strong that she deemed herself omnipotent, and was looking with lustful eyes towards England. Drake and Frobisher and Walter Raleigh were learning their lessons in seafaring; Elizabeth was Queen; while up at Warwickshire a barefoot boy named William Shakespeare was playing in the meadows, and romping in the lanes and alleys of Stratford ❧ ❧

All this was taking place at the time when

Jan Rubens was doing a little thinking on his own account. On reading the history of Europe, Flanders seems to one to have been a battle-ground from the dawn of history up to the night of June Eighteenth, Eighteen Hundred Fifteen, with a few incidental skirmishes since, for it is difficult to stop short. And it surely was meet that Napoleon should have gone up there to receive his Waterloo, and charge his cavalry into a sunken roadway, making a bridge across with a mingled mass of men and horses; upon which site now is a huge mound thrown up by the English, surmounted by a gigantic bronze lion cast from the captured cannon of the French ❧ ❧

Napoleon belonged to the Latin race: he pushed his rule North into Flanders, and there his prowess ended—there at the same place where Spanish rule had been throttled and turned back upon itself. "Thus far, and no farther." Jan Rubens was right. But he paid dearly for his prophecy.

¶ When William the Silent was away on his many warfaring expeditions, the man who had charge of certain of his affairs was Jan Rubens. Naturally this brought Rubens into an acquaintanceship with the wife of the silent prince. Rubens was a handsome man, ready in speech, and of the kind that makes friends easily. And if the wife of the Prince of Orange liked the vivacious Rubens better than the silent warrior (who won his sobriquet, they do say, through density of emotion and lack of ideas), why, who can blame her!

But Rubens had a wife of his own, to whom he was fondly attached; and this wife was also the close and trusted friend of the woman whose husband was off to the wars. And yet when this dense and silent man came back from one of his expeditions, it was only publicly to affront and disgrace his wife, and to cast Jan Rubens into a dungeon. No doubt the Prince was jealous of the courtly Rubens—and the Iagos are a numerous tribe. But Othello's limit had been reached. He damned the innocent woman to the lowest pit, and visited his wrath on the man.

Of course I know full well that all Northern Europe once rang with shrill gossip over the affair, and as usual the woman was declared the guilty party. Even yet, when topics for scandal in Belgium run short, this old tale is revived and gone over—sides being taken. I've gone over it, too, and although I may be in the minority, just as I possibly am as to the "guilt" of Eve, yet I stand firm on the side of the woman. I give the facts just as they appear, having canvassed the whole subject, possibly a little more than was good for me ❧ ❧

Republics may be ungrateful, but the favor of princes is fickle as the East Wind.

We make a fine hullabaloo nowadays because France or Russia occasionally tries and sentences a man without giving him an opportunity of defense; but in the Sixteenth Century the donjon-keeps of hundreds of castles in Europe were filled with prisoners whose offense consisted in being feared or disliked by some whimsical local ruler.

Jan Rubens was sent on an official errand to Dillenburg, and arriving there was seized and thrown into prison, without trial or the privilege of communicating with his friends ❧ ❧

Months of agonizing search on the part of his wife failed to find him, and the Prince only broke the silence long enough to usurp a woman's privilege by telling a lie, and declaring he did not know where Rubens was, "but I believe he has committed suicide through remorse."

The distracted wife made her way alone from prison to prison, and finally, by bribing an official, found her husband was in an underground cell in the fortress at Dillenburg. It was a year before she was allowed to communicate with or see him. But Maria Rubens was a true diplomat. You move a man not by going to him direct, but by finding out who it is that has a rope tied to his foot. She secured the help of the discarded wife of the Prince, and these two managed to interest a worthy bishop, who brought his influence to bear on Count John of Nassau. This man had jurisdiction of the district in which the fortress where Rubens was confined was located; and he agreed to release the prisoner on parole on condition that a deposit of six thousand thalers be left with him, and an agreement signed by the prisoner that he would give himself up when requested; and also, further, that he would acknowledge before witnesses that he was guilty of the charges made against him.

¶ The latter clause was to justify the Prince of Orange in his actions toward him.

Rubens refused to plead guilty, even for the sake of sweet liberty, on account of the smirch to the name of the Princess.

¶ But on the earnest request of both his wife and the "co-respondent," he finally accepted the terms in the same manner that Galileo declared the earth stood still

Rubens got his liberty, was loyal to his parole, but John of Nassau kept the six thousand thalers for "expenses."
¶ So much for the honor of princes; but in passing it is worthy of recall that Jan Rubens pleaded guilty of disloyalty to his wife, on request of said wife, in order that he might enjoy the society of said wife—and cast a cloud on the good name of another woman on said woman's request.

So here is a plot for a play: a tale of self-sacrifice and loyalty on the part of two women that puts to shame much small talk we hear from small men concerning the fickleness and selfishness of woman's love. "Brief as woman's love!" said Hamlet—but then, Hamlet was crazy.

Jan Rubens died in Cologne, March Eighteenth, Fifteen Hundred Eighty-seven, and lies buried in the Church of Saint Peter ❧ Above the grave is a slab containing this inscription: "Sacred to the memory of Jan Rubens, of Antwerp, who went into voluntary exile and retired with his family to Cologne, where he abode for nineteen years with his wife Maria, who was the mother of his seven children. With this his only wife Maria he lived happily for twenty-six years without any quarrel. This monument is erected by said Maria Pypelings Rubens to her sweetest and well-deserved husband."

Of course, no one knew then that one of the seven—the youngest son of Jan and Maria—was to win deathless fame, or that might have been carved on the slab, too, even if something else had to be omitted.

But Maria need not have added that last clause, stating who it was that placed the tablet: as it stands we should all have known that it was she who dictated the inscription. Epitaphs are proverbially untruthful; hence arose the saying, "He lies like an epitaph." The woman who can not evolve a good lie in defense of the man she loves is unworthy of the name of wife.

The lie is the weapon of defense that kind Providence provides for the protection of the oppressed. "Women are great liars," said Mahomet; "Allah in his wisdom made them so."

Hail, Maria Rubens! turned to dust these three hundred years, what star do you now inhabit? or does your avatar live somewhere here in this world? At the thought of your unselfish loyalty and precious fibbing, an army of valiant, ghostly knights will arise from their graves, and rusty swords leap from their scabbards if aught but good be said against thee ✤ ✤

"Ho, ho! and was n't your husband really guilty, and did n't you know it all the time?" I 'll fling my glove full in the face of any man who dare ask you such a question.

Beloved and loving wife for six-and-twenty years, and mother of seven, looking the world squarely in the eye and telling a large and beautiful untruth, carving it in marble to protect your husband's name, I kiss my hand to you!

ON the doorpost of a queer little stone house in Cologne is carved an inscription to the effect that Peter Paul Rubens was born there on June Twenty-ninth, Fifteen Hundred Seventy-seven. It is probably true that the parents of Rubens lived there, but Peter Paul was born at Siegen, under the shadow of a prison from which his father was paroled.

After a few years the discipline relaxed, for there were new prisoners coming along, and Maria and Jan were given permission to move to Cologne.

Peter Paul was ten years of age when his father died.

The next year the widow moved with her little brood back to Antwerp, back to the city from which her husband had been exiled just twenty years before. Five years previous the Prince of Orange, who had exiled her husband, was himself sent on a journey, via the dagger of an assassin ✤

As the chief enemy of Jan Rubens was dead, it was the hope of the widow to recover their property that had been confiscated ✤ ✤

Maria Rubens was a good Catholic; and she succeeded in making the authorities believe that her husband had been, too, for the home that Royalty had confiscated was returned to her ✤ ✤

The mother of Peter Paul loved the dim twilight mysteries of the Church, and accepted every dogma and edict as the literal word of God. It is easier and certainly safer to leave such matters to the specialists. She was a born diplomat. She recognized the power of the Church and knew that to win one must go with the current, not against it. To have doubts when the Church is willing to bear the whole burden, she thought very foolish. Had she been a man she would have been a leader among the Jesuits. The folly of opposition had been shown her most vividly in her husband's career. What could he not have been had he been wise and patient and ta'en the tide at its flood! And this was the spirit that she inculcated in the minds of her children.

Little Peter Paul was a handsome lad—handsome as his father—with big, dark brown eyes and clustering curls. He was bright, intelligent, and blessed with a cheerful, obliging disposition. He came into the world a welcome child, carrying the beauty of the morning in his face, and form, and spirit.

No wonder is it that the Countess de Lalaing desired the boy for a page as soon as she saw him. His mother embraced the opportunity to let her favorite child see court life, and so at the early age of twelve, at a plunge, he began that career in polite diplomacy that was to continue for half a century ✤ ✤

The Countess called herself his "other mother," and lavished upon him all the attention that a childless woman had to bestow. The mornings were sacred to his lessons, which were looked after by a Jesuit priest; and in the afternoon, another priest came to give the ladies lessons in the languages, and at these circles young Peter Paul was always present as one of the class.

Indeed, the earliest accomplishment of Peter Paul was his polyglot ability. When he arrived at Antwerp, a mere child, he spoke German, Flemish and French.

Such a favorite did little Peter Paul become with his "other mother," and her ladies of the court, that his sure-enough mother grew a bit jealous, and feared they would make a hothouse plant of her boy, and so she took him away.

The question was, for what profession should he be educated? That he should serve the Church and State was already a settled fact in the mother's mind: to get on in the world you must cultivate and wisely serve those who are in power— that is, those who have power to bestow ✣ Priests were plentiful as blackberries, and politicians were on every corner, and many of the priests and officeseekers had no special talent to recommend them. They were simply time-servers. Maria knew this: To get on you must have several talents, otherwise people will tire of you.

In Cologne, Maria Rubens had met returned pilgrims from Rome and they had told her of that trinity of giants, Michelangelo, Raphael and Leonardo; and how these men had been the peers of prince and pope, because they had the ability to execute marvelous works of beauty.

This talent called attention to themselves, so they were summoned out of the crowd and became the companions and friends of the greatest names of their time.

And then, how better can one glorify his Maker than by covering the sacred walls of temples with rich ornament!

¶ The boy entered into the project, and the mother's ambition that he should retrieve his father's fortune fired his heart. Thus does the failure in life of a parent often give incentive to the genius of a son.

Tobias Verhaecht was the man who taught Rubens the

elements of drawing, and inculcated into him that love of Nature which was to be his lifelong heritage. The word "landscape" is Flemish, and it was the Dutch who carried the term and the art into England. Verhaecht was among the very first of landscape-painters. He was a specialist: he could draw trees and clouds, and a winding river, but could not portray faces. And so he used to call in a worthy portrait-painter, by the name of Franck, to assist him whenever he had a canvas on the easel that demanded the human form. Then when Franck wanted background and perspective, Verhaecht would go over with a brush and a few pots of paint and help him out.

At fifteen, the keen, intuitive mind of Rubens had fathomed the talents of those two worthies, Verhaecht and Franck. His mind was essentially feminine: he absorbed ideas in the mass. Soon he prided himself on being able to paint alone as good a picture as the two collaborators could together. Yet he was too wise to affront them by the boast. The bent of his talent he thought was toward historical painting; and more than this, he knew that only epic art would open the churches for a painter. And so he next became a pupil under Adam van Noort. This man was a rugged old character, who worked out things in his own way and pushed the standard of painting full ten points to the front. His work shows a marked advance over that of his contemporaries and over the race of painters that preceded him. Every great artist is the lingering representative of an age that is dead, or else he is the prophet and forerunner of a golden age to come.

When I visited the Church of Saint Jaques in Antwerp, where Rubens lies buried, the good old priest who acted as guide called my attention to a picture by Van Noort, showing Peter finding the money in the mouth of the fish. "A close study of that picture will reveal to you the germ of the Rubens touch," said the priest, and he was surely right: its boldness of drawing, the strong, bright colors and the dexterity in handling all say, "Rubens." Rubens builded on the work of Van Noort.

Twenty years after Rubens had left the studio of Van Noort he paid tribute to his old master by saying, "Had Van Noort visited Italy and caught the spirit of the classicists, his name would stand first among Flemish artists."

Rubens worked four years with Van Noort and then entered the studio of Otto van Veen. This man was not a better painter than Van Noort, but he occupied a much higher social position, and Peter Paul was intent on advancing his skirmish-line. He never lost ground. Van Veen was Court Painter, and on friendly terms with the Archduke Albert, and Isabella, his wife, daughter of Philip the Second, King of Spain ❧ ❧

Van Veen took very few pupils—only those who had the ability to aid him in completing his designs. To have worked with this master was an introduction at once into the charmed circle of royalty.

Rubens was in no haste to branch out on his own account: he was quite content to know that he was gaining ground, making head upon the whole. He won the confidence of Van Veen at once by his skill, his cheerful presence, and ability to further the interests of his master and patrons ✤

In Fifteen Hundred Ninety-nine, when Rubens was twenty-two, he was enrolled as a free master at the Guild of Saint Luke on the nomination of Van Veen, who also about this time introduced the young artist to Albert and Isabella.

But the best service that Van Veen did for Rubens was in taking him into his home and giving him free access to the finest collection of Italian art in the Netherlands. These things filled the heart of Rubens with a desire to visit Italy, and there to dive deeply into the art spirit of that land from which all our art has sprung.

To go abroad then and gain access to the art treasures of the world was not a mere matter of asking for a passport, handing out a visiting-card, and paying your way.

Young men who wished to go abroad to study were required to pass a stiff examination. If it was believed that they could not represent their own country with honor, their passports were withheld. And to travel without a passport was to run the risk of being arrested as an absconder.

But Rubens' place in society was already secure. Instead of applying for his passports personally and undergoing the usual catechization, his desires were explained to Van Veen, and all technicalities were waived, as they always are when you strike the right man. Not only were the passports forthcoming, but Albert and Isabella wrote a personal note to Viccuzo Gonzaga, the Duke of Mantua, commending the young painter to the Duke's good offices.

Van Veen further explained to Rubens that to know the Duke of Mantua might mean either humiliation or crowning success. To attain the latter through the Duke of Mantua, it was necessary to make a good impression on Annibale Chieppo, the Duke's Minister of State ✤ Chieppo had the keeping of the ducal conscience as well as the key to the strong-box ✤ ✤

The Duke of Mantua was one of those strange loaded dice that Fate occasionally flings upon this checkerboard of time: one of those characters whose feverish faculties border on madness, yet who do the world great good by breaking up its balances, preventing social ankylosis, and eventually forcing upon mankind a new deal. But in the train of these vagrant stars famine and pestilence follow.

The Duke of Mantua was brother in spirit to the man who made Versailles—and making Versailles undid France.

Versailles is a dream: no language that the most enthusiastic lover of the beautiful may utter, can exaggerate the wonders of those acres of palaces and miles of gardens. The magnificence of the place makes the ready writer put up his pencil, and go away whipped, subdued and crestfallen to think that here are creations that no one pen can even catalog. Louis the Grand, we are told, had thirty-six thousand men and six thousand horses at work here at one time. No wonder Madame de Maintenon was oppressed by the treasures that were beyond the capacity of man to contemplate; and so off in the woods was built that lover's retreat, "The Trianon." And out there today, hidden in the forest, we behold the second Trianon, built by Marie Antoinette, and we also see those straw-thatched huts where the ladies of her Court played at peasant life.

Louis the Fourteenth builded so well that he discouraged his successor from doing anything but play keep-house, and so extensively that France was rent in twain, and so mightily that even Napoleon Bonaparte was staggered at the thought of maintaining Versailles.

"It's too much for any man to enjoy—I give it up!" said the Little Man, perplexed, and ordered every door locked and every window tightly shuttered. Then he placed a thousand men to guard the place and went about his business.

¶ But today Versailles belongs to the people of France; more, it belongs to the people of earth: all is free and you may carry away all the beauty of the place that your soul can absorb.

Now, who shall say that Louis the Fourteenth has not enriched the world?

The Duke of Mantua was sumptuous in his tastes, liberal, chivalrous, voluptuous, extravagant. At the same time he had a cultivated mind, an eye for proportion, and an ear for harmony. He was even pious at times, and like all debauchees had periods of asceticism. He was much given to gallantry, and his pension-list of beautiful women was not small. He was a poet and wrote some very good sonnets; he was a composer who sang, from his own compositions, after the wine had gone round; he was an orator who committed to memory and made his own the speeches that his secretary wrote.

He traveled much, and in great state, with a retinue of servants, armed guards, outriders and guides. Wherever he went he summoned the local poet, or painter, or musician, and made a speech to him, showing that he was familiar with his work by humming a tune or quoting a stanza. Then he put a chain of gold around the poor embarrassed fellow's neck, and a purse in his hands, and the people cheered ❧ ❧

When he visited a town, cavalcades met him afar out, and as he approached, little girls in white and boys dressed in velvet ran before and strewed flowers in front of his carriage ❧ ❧

Oh, the Duke of Mantua was a great man!

In his retinue was a troop of comedians, a court fool, two dwarfs for luck, seven cooks, three alchemists and an astrologer. Like the old woman who lived in a shoe, he had so many children he did n't know what to do. One of his sons married a princess of the House of Saxony, another son was a cardinal, and a daughter married into the House of Lorraine. He had alliances and close relations with every reigning family of Europe. The sister of his wife, Marie de' Medici, became "King of France," as Talleyrand avers, and had a mad, glad, sad, bad, jolly time of it.

Wherever the Duke of Mantua went, there too went Annibale Chieppo, the Minister of State. This man had a calm eye, a quiet pulse, and could locate any man or woman in his numerous retinue at any hour of the day or night. He was a diplomat, a soldier, a financier.

You could not reach the Duke until you had got past Chieppo.

¶ And the Duke of Mantua had much commonsense—for in spite of envy and calumny and threat he never lost faith in Annibale Chieppo.

No success in life is possible without a capable first-mate. Chieppo was king of first-mates.

He was subtle as Richelieu and as wise as Wolsey.

When Peter Paul Rubens, aged twenty-three, arrived at Venice, the Duke of Mantua and his train were there. Rubens presented his credentials to Chieppo, and the Minister of State read them, looked upon the handsome person of the young man, proved for himself he had decided talent as a painter, put him through a civil-service examination—and took him into favor. Such a young man as this, so bright, so courtly, so talented, must be secured. He would give the entire Court a new thrill.

"Tomorrow," said the Minister of State, "tomorrow you shall be received by the Duke of Mantua and his court!"

**T**HE ducal party remained at Venice for several weeks, and when it returned to Mantua, Rubens went along quite as a matter of course. From letters that he wrote to his brother Philip, as well as from many other sources, we know that the art colection belonging to the Duke of Mantua was very rich. It included works by the Bellinis, Correggio Leonardo da Vinci, Andrea del Sarto, Tintoretto, Titian, Paoli Veronese, and various others whose names have faded away like their colors.

Rubens had long been accustomed to the ways of polite society ✤ The magnificence of his manner, and the fine egotism he showed in his work, captivated the Court. The Duke was proud of his ward and paraded him before his artistic friends as the coming man, incidentally explaining that it was the Duke of Mantua who had made him and not he himself.

It was then the custom of those who owned masterpieces to have copies made and present them to various other lovers of the beautiful. If an honored guest was looking through your gallery, and expressed great pleasure in a certain canvas, the correct thing was to say, "I'll have my best painter make a copy of it, and send it to you"—and a memorandum was made on an ivory tablet. This gracious custom seems to have come down from the time when the owners of precious books constantly employed scribes and expert illuminators in making copies for distribution ✤ The work done in the scriptoriums of the monasteries, we know, was sent away as presents, or in exchange for other volumes.

Rubens set diligently to work copying in the galleries of

Mantua; and whether the Duke was happier because he had discovered Rubens than Rubens was because he had found the Duke, we do not know. Anyway, all that the young painter had hoped and prayed for had been sent him.

¶ Here was work from the very hands of the masters he had long worshiped from afar. His ambition was high and his strong animal spirits and tireless energy were a surprise to the easy-going Italians. The galleries were his without let or hindrance, save that he allow the ladies of the Court to come every afternoon and watch him work. This probably did not disturb him; but we find the experienced Duke giving the young Fleming some good advice, thus: "You must admire all these ladies in equal portion. Should you show favoritism for one, the rest will turn upon you; and to marry any one of them would be fatal to your art."

Rubens wrote the advice home to his mother, and the good mother viseed it and sent it back.

After six months of diligent work at Mantua we find Rubens starting for Rome with letters from the Duke to Cardinal Montalto, highly recommending him to the good graces of the Cardinal, and requesting, "that you will be graciously so good as to allow our Fleming to execute and make copies for us of such paintings as he may deem worthy."

Cardinal Montalto was a nephew of Pope Sixtus, and the strongest man, save the Pope, in Rome. He had immense wealth, great learning, and rare good sense in matters of art. He was a close friend of the Duke of Mantua; and to come into personal relationship with such a man was a piece of rare good fortune for any man.

The art world of Rome now belonged to Rubens—all doors opened at his touch. "Our Fleming" knew the value of his privileges. "If I do not succeed," he writes to his mother, "it will be because I have not improved my opportunities." The word fail was not in the Rubens lexicon.

His industry never relaxed. In Walpole's "Anecdotes of Painting," an account is given of a sketchbook that was compiled by Rubens at this time. The original sketchbook was in the possession of Maurice Johnson, of Spalding, England, in Eighteen Hundred Forty-five, at which time it was exhibited in London and attracted much attention.
¶ I have seen a copy of the book with its hundred or more sketches of the very figures that we now see and admire in the Uffizi and Pitti galleries and in the Vatican ✤ Eight generations of men have come and gone since Rubens sketched from the Old Masters, but there today stand the chiseled shapes, which were then centuries old, and there today are the "Titians" and the "Raphaellos" just as the exuberant Fleming saw them. Surely this must show us how short are the days of man! "Open then the door; you know how little while we have to stay!"

The two figures that seemed to impress Rubens most, as shown in the sketchbook, are the Farnese "Hercules" and Michelangelo's "David." He shows the foot of the "Hercules," and the hand of the "David," and gives front, back and side views with comments and criticisms. Then after a few pages have been covered by other matter he goes back again to the "Hercules"—the subject fascinates him ✤ ✤

When we view "The Crucifixion," in the Cathedral at Antwerp, we conclude that he admired the "Hercules" not wisely but too well, for the muscles stand out on all the figures, even of the Savior, in pure Farnese style. Two years after that picture was painted, he did his masterpiece, "The Descent From the Cross," and we behold with relief the change that had come over the spirit of his dreams. Mere pride in performing a difficult feat had given place to a higher motive. There is no reason to suppose that the Apostles had trained to perform the twelve labors of Hercules, or that the two Marys were Amazons. But the burly Roman forms went back to Flanders, and for many years staid citizens were slipped into classic attitudes to do duty as Disciples, Elders, Angels—all with swelling biceps, knotted muscles, and necks like the Emperor Vespasian.

The Mantuan Envoy at Rome had private orders from Chieppo to see that the Fleming was well treated. The Envoy was further requested to report to the Secretary how the painter spent his time, and also how he was regarded by Cardinal Montalto. Thus we see the wily Secretary set one servant watching another, and kept in close touch with all.

The reports, however, all confirmed the Secretary in his belief that the Fleming was a genius, and, moreover, worthy of all the encouragement that was bestowed upon him. The Secretary sent funds from time to time to the painter, with gentle hints that he should pay due attention to his behavior, and also to his raiment, for the apparel oft doth proclaim the man ✍ ✍

The Duke of Mantua seems to have regarded Rubens as

his own private property, and Rubens had too much sense to do anything by word or deed that might displease his patron ♣ ♣

When he had gotten all that Italy could give, or more properly all he could absorb, his intent was to follow his heart and go straight back to Flanders.

Three years had passed since Rubens had arrived in Venice—years of profit to both spirit and purse. He had painted pictures that placed him in the rank of acknowledged artists, and the Duke of Mantua had dropped all patronizing airs. With the ducal party Rubens had visited Verona, Florence, Pisa and Padua. His fame was more than local. The painter hinted to Chieppo that he would like to return to Antwerp, but the Secretary objected—he had important work for him.

**R**UBENS was from Flanders, and Flanders was a Spanish possession: then the Fleming knew the daughter of the King of Spain. No man was so well fitted to go on a delicate diplomatic mission to Spain as the Flemish painter. "You are my heart's jewel," said the Duke of Mantua to the Prime Minister, when the Minister suggested it ✢ ✢

The Duke wished private information as to certain things Spanish, and was also preparing the way to ask for sundry favors. The Court at Madrid was artistic in instinct; so was the Mantuan Court. To recognize the esthetic side of your friend's nature, when your friend is secretly not quite sure but that he is more worldly than spiritual, is a stroke of diplomacy. Spain was not really artistic, but there were stirrings being felt, and Velasquez and Murillo were soon to appear ✢ ✢

The Duke of Mantua wished to present the King of Spain with certain pictures; his mind was filled with a lively sense of anticipation of future favors to be received—which feeling we are told is gratitude. The entire ceremony must be carried out appropriately—the poetic unities being fully preserved. Therefore a skilful painter must be sent with the pictures, in order to see that they were safely transported, properly unpacked, and rightly hung.

Instructions were given to Peter Paul Rubens, the artistic ambassador, at great length, as to how he should proceed. He was to make himself agreeable to the King, and to one greater than the King—the man behind the throne—the Duke of Lerma; and to several fair ladies as well.

The pictures were copies of the masters—"Titians," "Raphaellos," "Tintorettos" and "Leonardos." They were copied with great fidelity, even to the signature and private marks of the original artist. In fact, so well was the work done that if the recipient inclined to accept them as originals, his mind must not be disabused. Further, the envoy was not supposed to know whether they were originals or not (even though he had painted them), and if worse came to worst he must say, "Well, surely they are just as good as the originals, if not better."

Presents were taken for a dozen or more persons. Those who were not so very artistic were to have gifts of guns, swords and precious stones. The ambassador was to travel in a new carriage, drawn by six horses and followed by wagons carrying the art treasures. All this so as to make the right impression and prove to Madrid that Mantua was both rich and generous ❦ And as a capsheaf to it all, the painter must choose an opportune moment and present his beautiful carriage and horses to the King, for the belief was rife that the King of Spain was really more horsey than artistic ❦ ❦

The pictures were selected with great care, and the finest horses to be found were secured, regardless of cost. Several weeks were consumed in preparations, and at last the cavalcade started away, with Rubens in the carriage and eleven velvet suits in his chest, as he himself has told us ❦ It was a long, hard journey to Madrid. There were encounters with rapacious landlords, and hairbreadth escapes in the imminent deadly custom-house. But in a month the chromatic diplomat arrived and entered Madrid at the head of his company, wearing one of the velvet suits, and riding a milk-white charger.

Rubens followed orders and wrote Signor Chieppo at great length, giving a minute account of every incident and detail of the journey and of his reception at Madrid. While at the Court he kept a daily record of happenings, which was also forwarded to the Secretary.

These many letters have recently been given to the public. They are in Italian, with a sprinkling here and there of good honest Dutch. All is most sincere, grave and explicit. Rubens deserved great credit for all these letters, for surely they were written with sweat and lamp-smoke. The work of the toiler is over all, but we must remember that at that time he had been studying Italian only about a year.

The literary style of Rubens was Johnsonese all his life, and he made his meaning plain only by repetitions and many rhetorical flounderings. Like the average sixteen-year-old boy who sits himself down and takes his pen in hand, all his sprightliness of imagination vanished at sight of an ink-bottle. With a brush his feelings were fluid, and in a company grace dwelt upon his lips; but when asked to write it out he gripped the pen as though it were a crowbar instead of a crow's-quill.

But Chieppo received his reports; and we know the embassy was a success—a great success. The debonair Fleming surprised the King by saying, "Your Majesty, it is like this"—and then with a few bold strokes drew a picture.

He modestly explained that he was not much of a painter

—"merely used a brush for his own amusement"—and then made a portrait for the Minister of State that exaggerated all of that man's good points, and ignored all his failings. There was a cast in the Minister's eye, but Ruben waived it. The Minister was delighted, and so was the King. He then made a portrait of the King that was as flattering as portraits should be that are painted for monarchs.

Among his other accomplishments the Fleming was a skilful horseman; he rode with such grace and dash that the King took him on his drives, Rubens riding by the side of the carriage, gaily conversing as they rode.

And so by the aid of his many talents he won the confidence of the King and Court and was initiated into the inner life of Spanish royalty in a way that Iberta, the Mantuan Resident, never had been. The King liked Rubens, and so did the Man behind the Throne ✣ ✣

Mortals do not merely like each other because they like each other; such a bond is tenuous as a spider's thread. I love you because you love the things that I love. One woman won my heart by her subtle appreciation of "The Dipsy Chanty." Men meet on a horse basis, a book basis, a religious basis, or some other mutual leaning; sometimes we find them uniting on a mutual dislike for something. For instance, I have a friend to whom I am bound by the tie of oneness because we dislike olives, and have a mutual indifference to the pretended claims of the unpronounceable Pole who wrote "Quo Vadis." The discovery was accidentally made in a hotel dining-room: we clasped hands across the board, and since then have been as brothers.

The more points at which you touch humanity the more friends you have—the greater your influence. Rubens was an artist, a horseman, a musician, a politician and a gourmet. When conceptions in the kitchen were vague, he would send for the cook and explain to him how to do it. He possessed a most discriminating palate and a fine appreciation of things drinkable. These accomplishments secured him a well-defined case of gout while yet a young man. He taught the Spanish Court how to smoke, having himself been initiated by an Englishman, who was a companion of Sir Walter Raleigh, and showed them how to roll a cigarette while engaged in ardent conversation. And the Spaniards have not yet lost the art, for once in Cadiz I saw a horse running away, and the driver rolled and lighted a cigarette before trying to stop the mad flight of the frantic brute.

In the Royal Gallery at Madrid are several large paintings by Rubens that were doubtless done at this time. They are religious subjects; but worked in, after the manner of a true diplomat, are various portraits of brave men and handsome women. To pose a worthy senator as Saint Paul, and a dashing lady of the Court as the Holy Virgin, was most gratifying to the phrenological development of approbativeness of the said senator and lady. Then, as the painter had pictured one, he must do as much for others, so there could be no accusation of favoritism.

Thus the months passed rapidly. The Duke of Lerma writes to Chieppo, "We desire your gracious permission to keep the Fleming another month, as very special portraits are required from his brush."

The extra month extended itself to three; and when at last Rubens started back for Mantua it was after a full year's absence ✤ ✤

The embassy was a most complete success. The diplomat well masked his true errand with the artist's garb: and who of all men was ever so well fitted by Nature to play the part as Rubens?

Yet he came near overdoing the part at least once. It was in this wise: he really was not sure that the honors paid him were on account of his being a painter or a courtier. But like comedians who think their forte is tragedy, so the part of courtier was more pleasing to Rubens than that of painter, because it was more difficult. He painted with such ease that he set small store on the talent: it was only a makeshift for advancement.

Don John, Duke of Braganza, afterward King of Portugal, was a lover of art, and desired to make the acquaintance of the painter. So he wrote to Rubens at Madrid, inviting him to Villa Vitiosa, his place of residence.

Rubens knew how the Duke of Mantua did these things—he decided to follow suit.

With a numerous train, made up from the fringe of the Madrid Court, with hired horsemen going before, and many servants behind, the retinue started away. Coming within five miles of the villa of Don John, word was sent that Rubens and his retinue awaited his embassy.

Now Don John was a sure-enough duke and could muster quite a retinue of his own on occasion, yet he had small taste for tinsel parades. Men who have a real good bank-balance do not have to wear fashionable clothes. Don John was a plain, blunt man who liked books and pictures. He wanted to see the painter, not a courtier: and when he heard of the style in which the artist was coming, he just put a boy on a donkey and sent word out that he was not at home. And further, to show the proud painter his place, he sent along a small purse of silver to pay the artist for the trouble to which he had been. The rebuke was so delicate that it was altogether lost on Rubens—he was simply enraged.

IN all, Rubens spent eight years in the service of the Duke of Mantua. He had visited the chief cities of Italy, and was familiar with all the art of the golden ages that had gone before. When he left Italy he had to take advantage of the fact that the Duke was in France, for every time before, when he had suggested going, he was questioned thus: "Why, have you not all you wish? What more can be done for you? Name your desire and you shall have it."

But Rubens wanted home: Antwerp, his mother, brothers, sister, the broad River Scheldt, and the good old Flemish tongue ♣ ♣

Soon after arriving in Antwerp he was named as Court Painter by Albert and Isabella. Thus he was the successor of his old master, Van Veen.

He was now aged thirty-two, in possession of an income from the State, and a fame and name to be envied. He was rich in money, jewels and art treasures brought from Italy, for he had the thrifty instincts of a true Dutchman.

And it was a gala day for all Antwerp when the bells rang and the great organ in the Cathedral played the wedding-march when Peter Paul Rubens and Isabella Brandt were married, on the Thirteenth of October, Sixteen Hundred Nine. Never was there a happier mating.

That fine picture at Munich of Rubens and his wife tells of the sweet comradeship that was to be theirs for many years. He opened a school, and pupils flocked to him from all Europe; commissions for work came and orders for altar-pieces from various churches.

An order was issued by the Archduke that he should not leave Holland, and a copy of the order was sent to the Duke of Mantua, to shut off his importunities.

Among the pupils of Rubens we find the name of Jordaens (whom he had first known in Italy), De Crayer, Antony van Dyck, Franz Snyder and many others who achieved distinction. Rubens was a positive leader; so animated was his manner that his ambition was infectious. All his young men painted just as he did. His will was theirs. From now on, out of the thousands of pictures signed "P. P. Rubens," we can not pick out a single picture and say, "Rubens did this." He drew outlines and added the finishing touches; and surely would not have signed a canvas of which he did not approve. In his great studio at Antwerp, at various times, fully a hundred men worked to produce the pictures we call "Rubens."

Those glowing canvases in the "Rubens Gallery" of the Louvre, showing the history and apotheosis of Marie de' Medici, were painted at Antwerp. The joyous, exuberant touch of Rubens is over all, even though the work was done by 'prentice hands.

Peaceful lives make dull biographies, and in prosperity is small romance.

We may search long before finding a life so full to overflowing of material good things as that of Rubens. All he touched turned to gold. From the time he returned to Antwerp in Sixteen Hundred Eight to his death in Sixteen Hundred Forty, his life-journey was one grand triumphal march ❧ ❧

His many diplomatic missions were simply repetitions of his first Spanish embassy, with the Don John incident left out, for Don John seems to have been the only man who was not at home to the gracious Rubens.

Mr. Ruskin has said: "Rubens was a great painter, but he lacked that last undefinable something which makes heart speak to heart. You admire, but you never adore. No real sorrow ever entered his life."

Perhaps we get a valuable clue in that last line. Great art is born of feeling, and the heart of Rubens was never touched by tragedy, nor the rocky fastnesses of his tears broken in upon by grief. In many ways his was the spirit of a child: he had troubles, but not sufficient to prevent refreshing sleep, and when he awoke in the morning the trials of yesterday were gone ✣ ✣

Even when the helpful, faithful and loving Isabella Brandt was taken away from him by death, there soon came other joys to take the place of those that were lost.

We have full fifty pictures of his second wife: she looks down at us—smiling, buxom, content—from every gallery-wall in Europe. Rubens was fifty-three and she was sixteen when they were married, and were it not for a twinge of gout now and then, he would have been as young as she.

¶ When Rubens went to England on "an artistic commission," we see that he captured Charles the First just as he captured the court of Spain. He painted five portraits of the King that we can trace ✣ The mild-mannered Charles was greatly pleased with the fine portrait of himself bestriding the prancing cream-colored charger.

Several notable artists, Sir Joshua Reynolds among them, have complimented the picture by taking the horse, background and pose, and placing another man in the saddle—or more properly, taking off the head of Charles the First and putting on the head of any bold patron who would furnish the price. In looking through the galleries of Europe, keep your eye out for equestrian portraits, and you will be surprised to see on your tab when you have made the rounds, how many painters have borrowed that long-maned, yellow horse that still rears in the National Gallery in London, smelling the battle afar off—as Charles himself preferred to smell it.

Rubens had a good time in England, although his patience was severely tried by being kept at painting for months, awaiting an opportune time to give King Charles some good advice on matters political.

English ways were very different from those of the Continent, but Rubens soon spoke the language with fluency, even if not with precision.

Rubens spoke seven languages, and to speak seven languages is to speak no one well. On this point we have a little comment from high authority. Said Charles the First, writing to Buckingham, "The Fleming painter prides himself on being able to pass for an Englishman, but his English is so larded with French, Dutch and Italian that we think he must have been employed on the Tower of Babel."

While painting the ceiling of the banqueting-room at Whitehall (where a Dutchman was later to be crowned King of England), he discussed politics with the Duke of Buckingham and the King from the scaffold. Some years after we find Buckingham visiting Rubens at his home in Antwerp, dickering for his fine collection of curios and paintings.

The Duke afterwards bought the collection and paid Rubens ten thousand pounds in gold for it.

Every one complimented Rubens on his shrewdness in getting so much money for the wares, and Rubens gave a banquet to his friends in token of the great sale to the Britisher. It was a lot of money, to be sure, but the Englishman realized the worth of the collection better than Rubens. We have a catalog of the collection. It includes nineteen Titians, thirteen Paul Veroneses, seventeen Tintorettos, three Leonardos, three Raphaels and thirteen pictures by Rubens himself.

A single one of the Titians, if sold at auction today, would bring more than the Duke paid for the entire collection.

James McNeil Whistler has said, "There may be a doubt about Rubens having been a Great Artist; but he surely was an Industrious Person."

There is barely enough truth in Mr. Whistler's remark, taken with its dash of wit, to save it; but Philip Gilbert Hamerton's sober estimate is of more value: "The influence of Rubens for good can not be overestimated. He gave inspiration to all he met, and his example of industry, vivid imagination, good-cheer and good taste have had an incalculable influence on art. We have more canvases from his hand than from the hand of any other master. And these pictures are a quarry to which every artist of today, consciously or unconsciously, is indebted."

MEISSONIER

MEISSONIER

# MEISSONIER

I NEVER hesitate about scraping out the work of days, and beginning afresh, so as to satisfy myself, and try to do better. Ah! that "better" which one feels in one's soul, and without which no true artist is ever content! ¶ Others may approve and admire; but that counts for nothing, compared with one's own feeling of what ought to be.—Meissonier's "Conversations."

# MEISSONIER

LIFE in this world is a collecting, and all the men and women in it are collectors. ¶ The question is, What will you collect? Most men are intent on collecting dollars. Their waking-hours are taken up with inventing plans, methods, schemes, whereby they may secure dollars from other men. To gather as many dollars as possible, and to give out as few, is the desideratum. But when you collect one thing you always incidentally collect others. The fisherman who casts his net for shad usually secures a few other fish, and once in a while a turtle, which enlarges the mesh to suit, and gives sweet liberty to the shad. To focus exclusively on dollars is to secure jealousy, fear, vanity, and a vaulting ambition that may claw its way through the mesh and let your dollars slip into the yeasty deep.

Ragged Haggard and his colleague, Cave-of-the-Winds, collect bacteria; while the fashionable young men of the day, with a few exceptions, are collecting headaches, regrets, weak nerves, tremens, paresis—death. Of course we shall all die (I will admit that), and further, we may be a long time dead (I will admit that), and moreover, we may be going through the world for the last time—as to that I do not know; but while we are here it seems the part of reason to devote our energies to collecting that which brings as much quiet joy to ourselves, and as little annoyance to others, as possible.

My heart goes out to the collector. In the soul of the collector of old books, swords, pistols, brocades, prints, clocks and bookplates, there is only truth. If he gives you his friendship, it is because you love the things that he loves; he has no selfish wish to use your good name to further his own petty plans—he only asks that you shall behold, and beholding, your eye shall glow, and your heart warm within you.

Inasmuch as we live in the age of the specialist, one man often collects books on only one subject, Dante for instance; another, nothing but volumes printed at Venice; another, works concerning the stage; and still another devotes all his spare time to securing tobacco-pipes. And I am well aware that the man who for a quarter of a century industriously collects snuffboxes has a supreme contempt for the man who collects both snuffboxes and clocks. And in this does the specialist reveal that his normal propensity to collect has degenerated. That is to say, it has refined itself into an abnormality, and from the innocent desire to collect, has shifted off into a selfish wish to outrival.

The man who collects many things, with easy, natural leanings toward, say, spoons, is pure in heart and free from guile; but when his soul centers on spoons exclusively, he has fallen from his high estate and is simply possessed of a lust for ownership—he wants to own more peculiar spoons than any man on earth. Such a one stirs up wrath and rivalry, and is the butt and byword of all others who collect spoons.

¶ Prosperous, practical, busy people sometimes wonder why other folks build cabinets with glass fronts and strong locks and therein store postage-stamps, bits of old silks, autographs and books that are very precious only when their leaves are uncut; and so I will here endeavor to explain ✄ At the same time I despair of making my words intelligible to any but those who are collectors, or mayhap to those others who are in the varioloid stage.

Then possibly you say I had better not waste good paper and ink by recording the information, since collectors know already, and those who are without the pale have neither eyes to see nor hearts to incline. But the simple fact is, the proposition that you comprehend on first hearing was yours already; for how can you recognize a thing as soon as it comes into view if you have never before seen it? You have thought my thought yourself, or else your heart would not beat fast and your lips say, "Yes, yes!" when I voice it. Truth is in the air, and when your head gets up into the right stratum of atmosphere you breathe it in. You may not know that you have breathed it in until I come along and write it out on this blank sheet, and then you read it and say, "Yes—your hand! that is surely so; I knew it all along!"

And so then if I tell you a thing you already know, I confer on you the great blessing of introducing you to yourself and of giving you the consciousness that you know.

And to know you know is power. And to feel the sense of power is to feel a sense of oneness with the Source of Power.

Let's see—what was it, then, that we were talking about? Oh, yes! collectors and collecting.

Men collect things because these things stir imagination and link them with the people who once possessed and used these things. Thus, through imagination, is the dead past made again to live and throb and pulse with life. Man is not the lonely creature that those folks with bad digestions sometimes try to have us believe.

We are brothers not only to all who live, but to all who have gone before.

And so we collect the trifles that once were valuables for other men, and by the possession of these trifles are we bounden to them. These things stimulate imagination, stir the sympathies, and help us forget the cramping bounds of time and space that so often hedge us close around.

The people near us may be sordid, stupid, mean; or more likely they are weary and worn with the battle for mere food, shelter and raiment; or they are depressed by that undefined brooding fear which civilization exacts as payment for benefits forgot—so their better selves are subdued.

But through fancy's flight we can pick our companions out of the company of saints and sinners who have long turned to dust. I have the bookplates of Holbein and Hogarth, and I have a book once owned by Rembrandt, and so I do not say Holbein and Hogarth and Rembrandt were—I say they are ❧ ❧

And thus the collector confuses the glorious dead and the living in one fairy company; and although he may detect varying degrees of excellence, for none does he hold contempt, of none is he jealous, none does he envy. From them he asks nothing, upon him they make no demands.

In the collector's cast of mind there is something very childlike and ingenuous.

My little girl has a small box of bright bits of silk thread that she hoards very closely; then she possesses certain pieces of calico, nails, curtain-rings, buttons, spools and fragments of china—all of which are very dear to her heart. And why should they not be? For with them she creates a fairy world, wherein are only joy, and peace, and harmony, and light—quite an improvement on this! Yes, dearie, quite.

**M**EISSONIER, the artist, began collecting very early. He has told us that he remembers, when five years of age, of going with his mother to market and collecting rabbits' ears and feet, which he would take home, and carefully nail up on the wall of the garret. And it may not be amiss to explain here that the rabbit's foot as an object of superstitious veneration has no real place outside of the United States of America, and this only South of Mason and Dixon's line.

The Meissonier lad's collection of rabbits' ears increased until he had nearly colors enough to run the chromatic scale. Then he collected pigeons' wings in like manner, and if you have ever haunted French market-places you know how natural a thing this would be for a child. The boy's mother took quite an interest in his amusements, and helped him to spread the wings out and arrange the tails fan-shape on the walls. They had long strings of buttons and boxes of spools in partnership; and when they would go up the Seine on little excursions on Sunday afternoons, they would bring back rich spoils in the way of swan feathers, butterflies, "snake-feeders" and tiny shells. Then once they found a bird's nest, and as the mother bird had deserted it, they carried it home. That was a red-letter day, for the garret collection had increased to such an extent that a partition was made across the corner of a room by hanging up a strip of cloth. And all the things in that corner belonged to Ernest —his mother said so.

Ernest's mother seems to have had a fine, joyous, childlike nature, so she fully entered into the life of her boy. He wanted no other companion. In fact, this mother was little better herself than a child in years—she was only sixteen when she bore him. They lived at Lyons then, but three years later moved to Paris. Her temperament was poetic, religious, and her spirit had in it a touch of superstition—which is the case with all really excellent women.

But this sweet playtime was not for long—the mother died in Eighteen Hundred Twenty-five, aged twenty-four years.

¶ I suppose there is no greater calamity that can befall a child than to lose his mother. Still, Nature is very kind, and for Ernest Meissonier there always remained firm, clear-cut memories of a slight, fair-haired woman, with large open gray eyes, who held him in her arms, sang to him, and rocked him to sleep each night as the darkness gathered. He lived over and over again those few sunshiny excursions up the river; and he knew all the reeds and flowers and birds she liked best, and the places where they had landed from the boat and lunched together were forever to him sacred spots.

¶ But the death of his mother put a stop for a time to his collecting. The sturdy housekeeper who came to take the mother's place, speedily cleared "the truck" out of the corner, and forbade the bringing of any more feathers and rabbits' feet into her house—well, I guess so! The birds' nests, long grasses, reeds, shells and pigeons' wings were tossed straightway into the fireplace, and went soaring up the chimney in smoke.

The destruction of the collection did n't kill the propensity to collect, however, any more than you can change a man's opinions by burning his library. It only dampened the desire for a time. It broke out again after a few years and continued for considerably more than half a century. There was a house at Poissy "full to the roof-tiles" of books, marbles, bronzes and innumerable curios, gathered from every corner of the earth; and a palace at Paris filled in like manner, for which Ernest Meissonier had expended more than a million francs.

¶ In the palace at Paris, when the owner was near his three-score years and ten, he took from a locker a morocco case, and opening it, showed his friend, Dumas, a long curl of yellow hair; and then he brought out a curious old white-silk dress, and said to the silent Dumas, "This curl was cut from my mother's head after her death, and this dress was her wedding-gown."

A few days after this Meissonier wrote these words in his journal: "It is the Twentieth of February—the morning of my seventieth birthday. What a long time to look back upon! This morning, at the hour when my mother gave me birth, I wished my first thoughts to be of her. Dear Mother, how often have the tears risen to my eyes at the remembrance of you! It was your absence—the longing I had for you—that made you so dear to me. The love of my heart goes out to you! Do you hear me, Mother, calling and crying for you? How sweet it must be to have a mother, I say to myself."

# MEISSONIER

"I WOULD have every man rich," said Emerson, "that he might know the worthlessness of riches."

Every man should have a college education, in order to show him how little the thing is really worth. The intellectual kings of the earth have seldom been college-bred. Napoleon ever regretted the lack of instruction in his early years; and in the minds of such men as Abraham Lincoln and Ernest Meissonier there usually lingers the suspicion that they have dropped something out of their lives ❧ ❧

"I'm not a college man—ask Seward," said Lincoln, when some one questioned him as to the population of Alaska. The remark was merry jest, of course, but as in all jest there lurks a grain of truth, so did there here.

At the height of Meissonier's success, when a canvas from his hand commanded a larger price than the work of any other living artist, he exclaimed, "Oh, if only I had been given the advantages of a college training!"

If he had, it is quite probable that he never would have painted better than his teacher. Discipline might have reduced his daring genius to neutral salts, and taken all that fine audacity from his brush.

He was a natural artist: he saw things clearly and in detail; he had the heart to feel, and he longed for the skill to express that which he saw and felt. And when the desire is strong enough it brings the thing—and thus is prayer answered ❧ Meissonier while but a child set to work making pictures— he declared he would be an artist. And in spite of his father's attempts to shame him out of his whim, and to starve him into a more practical career, his resolution stuck.

He worked in a drugstore and drew on the wrapping-paper; then with this artist a few days and then with that. He tried illustrating, and finally a bold stand was made and a little community formed that decided on storming the Salon.

There is something pathetic in that brotherhood of six young men, binding themselves together, swearing they would stand together and aid each other in producing great art.

The dead seriousness of the scheme has a peculiar sophomore quality. There were Steinheil, Trimolet, Daumier, Daubigny, Deschaumaes and Meissonier, all aged about twenty, strong, sturdy, sincere and innocently ignorant—all bound they would be artists.

Two of these young men were sign-painters, the others did odd jobs illustrating, and filled in the time at anything which chance offered. When one got an invitation out to dinner he would go, and furtively drop biscuit and slices of meat into his lap, and then slyly transfer them to his waistcoat-pockets, so as to take them to his less fortunate brethren.

¶ They haunted the galleries, made themselves familiar with catalogs, criticized without stint, knew all about current prices, and were able to point out the great artists of Paris when they passed proudly up the street.

They sketched eternally, formed small wax models, and made great preparations for masterpieces.

The reason they did not produce the masterpieces was because they did not have money to buy brushes, paints and canvas. Neither did they have funds to purchase food to last until the thing was done; and it is difficult to produce great art on half-rations. So they formed the brotherhood, and one midnight swore eternal fealty. They were to draw lots: the lucky member was to paint and the other five were to support him for a month. He was to be supplied his painting outfit and to be absolutely free from all responsibility as to the bread-and-butter question for a whole month.

Trimolet was the first lucky man.

He set diligently to work, and dined each evening on a smoking mutton-chop with a bottle of wine, at a respectable restaurant. The five stood outside and watched him through the window—they dined when and where they could.

His picture grew apace, and in three weeks was completed. It was entitled, "Sisters of Charity Giving Out Soup to the Poor." The work was of a good machine-made quality, not good enough to praise nor bad enough to condemn: it was like Tomlinson of Berkeley Square.

On account of the peculiar subject with which it dealt, it found favor with a worthy priest, who bought it and presented it to a convent.

This so inflated Trimolet that he suggested it would be a good plan to keep right on with the arrangement, but the five objected.

Steinheil was next appointed to feed the vestal fire. His picture was so-so, but would not sell.

Daubigny came next, and lived so high that inspiration got clogged, fatty degeneration of the cerebrum set in, and after a week he ceased to paint—doing nothing but dream.

When the turn of the fourth man came, Meissonier had concluded that the race must be won by one and one, and his belief in individualism was further strengthened by an order for a group of family portraits, with a goodly retainer in advance.

Straightway he married Steinheil's sister, with whom he had been some weeks in love, and the others feeling aggrieved that an extra mouth to feed, with danger of more, had been added to the "Commune," declared the compact void.

Trimolet still thought well of the arrangement, though, and agreed, if Meissonier would support him, to secure fame and fortune for them both.

Meissonier declined the offer with thanks, and struck boldly out on his own account.

The woman who had so recklessly agreed to share his poverty must surely have had faith in him—or are very young people who marry incapable of either faith or reason? Never mind; she did not hold the impulsive young man back.

She could n't—nothing but death could have stayed such ambition. His will was unbending and his ambition never tired ✿ ✿

He was an athlete in strength, and was fully conscious that to be a good animal is the first requisite. He swam, rowed, walked, and could tire out any of his colleagues at swordplay or skittles.

But material things were scarce those first few years of married life, and once when the table had bread, but no meat nor butter, he took the entire proceeds of a picture and purchased a suit of clothing of the time of Louis the Grand: not to wear, of course—simply to put in the "collection."

Small wonder is it that, for some months after, when he

would walk out alone the fond wife would caution him thus: "Now Ernest, do not go through that old-clothes market—you know your weakness."

"I have no money, so you need not worry," he would gaily reply ❧ ❧

Of those times of pinching want he has written, "As to happiness—is it possible to be wretched at twenty, when one has health, a passion for art, free passes for the Louvre, an eye to see, a heart to feel, and sunshine gratis?"

But poverty did not last long. Pictures such as this young man produced must attract attention anywhere. He belonged to no school, but simply worked away after his own fashion; what he was bound to do was to produce a faithful picture—sure, clear, strong, vivid. He saw things clearly and his sympathies were acute, as is shown in every canvas he produced ❧ ❧

Meissonier had the true artistic conscience—he was incapable of putting out an average, unobjectionable picture—it must have positive excellence. "There is a difference," said he, "between a successful effort and a work of love." He painted only in the loving mood.

No greater blessing than the artistic conscience can come to any worker in art, be he sculptor, writer, singer or painter. Hold fast to it, and it shall be your compass in time when the sun is darkened. To please the public is little, but to satisfy your Other Self, that self that looks over your shoulder and watches your every thought and deed, is much. No artistic success worth having is possible unless you satisfy that Other Self ❧ ❧

But like the moral conscience it can be dallied with until the grieved spirit turns away, and the wretch is left to his fate.
¶ Meissonier never hesitated to erase a whole picture when it did not satisfy his inward sense—customers might praise and connoisseurs offer to buy, it made no difference. "I have some one who is more difficult to please than you," he would say; "I must satisfy myself."

The fine intoxication that follows good artistic work is the highest joy that mortals ever know. But once let a creative artist lower his standard and give the world the mere product of his brain, with heart left out, that man will hate himself for a year and a day. He has sold his soul for a price: joy has flown, and bitterness is his portion. Meissonier never trifled with his compass. To the last he headed for the polestar.

**M**EISSONIER'S early domestic affairs can best be guessed from his oft-repeated assertion that the artist should never marry. "To produce great work, Art must be your mistress," he said. "You must be married to your work. A wife demands unswerving loyalty as her right, and a portion of her husband's time she considers her own. This is proper with every profession but that of Art. The artist must not be restrained, nor should even a wife come between him and his Art. The artist must not be judged by the same standards that are made for other men. Why? Simply because when you begin to tether him you cramp his imagination and paralyze his hand. The priest and artist must not marry, for it is too much to expect any woman to follow them in their flight, and they have no moral right to tie themselves to a woman and then ask her to stay behind."

¶ From this and many similar passages in the "Conversations" it is clear that Meissonier had no conception of the fact that a woman may possibly keep step with her mate. He simply never considered such a thing.

A man's opinions concerning womankind are based upon the knowledge of the women he knows best.

We can not apply Hamerton's remark concerning Turner to Meissonier. Hamerton said that throughout Turner's long life he was lamentably unfortunate in that he never came under the influence of a strong and good woman.

Meissonier associated with good women, but he never knew one with a spread of spiritual wing sufficient to fit her to be his companion. There is a minor key of loneliness and heart hunger running through his whole career. Possibly, in the wisdom of Providence, this was just what he needed to urge him on to higher and nobler ends. He never knew peace, and the rest for which he sighed slipped him at the very last. "I'm tired, so tired," he sighed again and again, in those later years, when he had reached the highest pinnacle.

And still he worked—it was his only rest!

Meissonier painted very few pictures of women, and in some miraculous way skipped that stage in esthetic evolution wherein most artists affect the nude. In his whole career he never produced a single "Diana," nor a "Susanna at the Bath." He had no artistic sympathy with "Leda and the Swan," and once when Delaroche chided him for painting no pictures of women, he was so ungallant as to say, "My dear fellow, men are much more beautiful than women!"

¶ During the last decade of his life Meissonier painted but one portrait of a woman, and to America belongs the honor. The sitter was Mrs. J. W. Mackay, of California.

As all the world knows, Mrs. Mackay refused to accept the canvas. She declared the picture was no likeness, and further, she would not have it for a gift.

"So you do not care for the picture?" asked the great artist.

¶ "Me? Well, I guess not—not that picture!"

"Very well, Madam, I think—I think I'll keep it for myself. I'll place it on exhibition!" And the great artist looked out of the window in an absent-minded way, and hummed a tune ✤ ✤

This put another phase on the matter. Mrs. Mackay winced, and paid the price, which rumor says was somewhere between ten and twenty-five thousand dollars. ✤ She took the little canvas in her carriage and drove away with it, and what became of the only portrait of a woman painted by Meissonier during his later years, nobody knew but Mrs. Mackay, and Mrs. Mackay never told.

Meissonier once explained to a friend that his offense consisted in producing a faithful likeness of the customer.

The Mackay incident did not end when the lady paid the coin and accepted the goods. Meissonier, by the haughtiness of his manner, his artistic independence, and most of all, by his unpardonable success, had been sowing dragons' teeth for half a century. And now armed enemies sprang up, and sided with the woman from California. They made it an international episode: less excuses have involved nations in war in days agone. But the enemies of Meissonier did not belong alone to America, although here every arm was braced and every tongue wagged to vindicate the cause of our countrywoman.

In Paris the whole art world was divided into those who sided with Meissonier and those who were against him. Cafes echoed with the sounds of wordy warfare; the columns of all magazines and newspapers bulged with heated argument; newsboys cried extras on the street, and bands of students paraded the boulevards singing songs in praise of Mrs. Mackay and in dishonor of Meissonier, "the pretender." The assertion was made again and again that Meissonier had fed sham art upon the public, and by means of preposterous prices and noisy puffing had hypnotized a world. They called him the artist of the Infinitely Little, King of Lilliput, and challenged any one to show where he had thrown heart and high emotion into his work. Studies of coachmen, smokers, readers, soldiers, housemaids, chess-players, cavaliers and serenaders were not enough upon which to base an art reputation—the man must show that he had moved men to high endeavor, said the detractors. A fund was started to purchase the Mackay portrait, so as to do the very thing that Meissonier had threatened to do, but dare not: place the picture on exhibition. To show the picture, the enemy said, would be to prove the artist's commonplace quality, and not only this, but it would prove the man a rogue. They declared he was incapable of perceiving the good qualities in a sitter, and had consented for a price to portray a person whom he disliked; and as a result, of course, had produced a caricature; and then had blackmailed his patron into paying an outrageous sum to keep the picture from the public ﴾ ﴿

The argument sounded plausible. And so the battle raged, just as it has since in reference to Zola.

The tide of Meissonier's prosperity began to ebb: prospective buyers kept away; those who had given commissions canceled them.

Meissonier's friends saw that something must be done. They inaugurated a "Meissonier Vindication," by making an exhibition of one hundred fifty-five "Meissoniers"—and the public was invited to come and be the jury. Art-lovers from England went in bodies, and all Paris filed through the gallery, as well as a goodly portion of provincial France. By the side of each canvas stood a gendarme to protect it from a possible fanatic whose artistic hate could not be restrained.

To a great degree this exhibition brought feeling to a normal condition. Meissonier was still a great artist, yet he was human and his effects were now believed to be gotten by natural methods. But there was a lull in the mad rush to secure his wares. The Vanderbilts grew lukewarm; titled connoisseurs from England were not so anxious; and Mrs. Mackay sat back and smiled through her tears.

Meissonier had expended over a million francs on his house in the Boulevard Malesherbes in Paris, and nearly as much on the country-seat at Poissy. These places were kingly in their appointments and such as only the State should attempt to maintain. For a single man, by the work of his right hand, to keep them up was too much to expect.

Meissonier's success had been too great. As a collector he had overdone the thing. Only poor men, or those of moderate incomes, should be collectors, for then the joy of sacrifice is theirs. Charles Lamb's covetous looking on the book when it was red, daily for months, meanwhile hoarding his pay, and at last one Saturday night swooping down and carrying the volume home to Bridget in triumph, is the true type ✧ But money had come to Meissonier by hundreds of thousands of francs, and often sums were forced upon him as advance payments. He lived royally and never imagined that his hand and brain could lose their cunning, or the public be fickle ✧ The fact that a "vindication" had been necessary was galling: the great man grew irritable and his mood showed itself in his work: his colors grew hard and metallic, and there were angles in his lines where there should have been joyous curves.

Debts began to press. He painted less and busied his mind with reminiscence—the solace of old age.

And then it was that he dictated to his wife the "Conversations." The book reveals the quality of his mind with rare fidelity—and shows the power of this second wife fully to comprehend him. And thus did she disprove some of the unkind philosophy given to the world by her liege. But the talk in the "Conversations" is of an old man in whose heart was a tinge of bitterness. Yet the thought is often lofty and the comment clear and full of flashing insight. It is the book of Ecclesiastes over again, written in a minor key, with a little harmless gossip added for filling. Meissonier died in Eighteen Hundred Ninety-one, aged seventy-six years.

THE canvas known as "Eighteen Hundred Seven," which is regarded as Meissonier's masterpiece, has a permanent home in the Metropolitan Museum of Art in New York. The central figure is Napoleon, at whose shrine the great artist loved to linger. The "Eighteen Hundred Seven" occupied the artist's time and talent for fifteen years, and was purchased by A. T. Stewart for sixty thousand dollars. After Mr. Stewart's death his art treasures were sold at auction, and this canvas was bought by Judge Henry Hilton and presented to the city of New York.

There are in all about seventy-five pictures by Meissonier owned in America. Several of his pieces are in the Vanderbilt collection, others are owned by collectors in Chicago, Cleveland and Saint Louis.

There are various glib sayings to the effect that the work of great men is not appreciated until after they are dead. This may be so and it may not. It depends upon the man and the age. Meissonier enjoyed full half a century of the highest and most complete success that was ever bestowed upon an artist.

The strong intellect and marked personality of the man won him friends wherever he chose to make them; and it probably would have been better for his art if a degree of public indifference had been his portion in those earlier years. His success was too great: the calm judgment of posterity can never quite endorse the plaudits paid the living man. He is one of the greatest artists the Nineteenth Century has produced, but that his name can rank among the great artists of all time is not at all probable.

William Michael Rossetti has summed the matter up well by saying: "Perfection is so rare in this world that when we find it we must pause and pay it the tribute of our silent admiration. It is easy to say that Meissonier should have put in this and omitted that. Had he painted differently he would have been some one else. The work is faultless, and such genius as he showed must ever command the homage of those who know by experience the supreme difficulty of having the hand materialize the conceptions of the mind. And yet Meissonier's conceptions outmatched his brush: he was greater than his work. He was a great artist, and better still, a great man—proud, frank, fearless and conscientious."

THE NEW YORK
PUBLIC LIBRARY

ASTOR, LENOX AND
TILDEN FOUNDATIONS
R          L

TITIAN

AN

# TITIAN

TITIAN by a few strokes of the brush knew how to make the general image and character of whatever object he attempted. His great care was to preserve the masses of light and shade, and to give by opposition the idea of that solidity which is inseparable from natural objects. He was the greatest of the Venetians, and deserves to rank with Raphael and Michelangelo.—Sir Joshua Reynolds.

# TITIAN

HE march of progress and the rage for improvement make small impression on Venice. The cabmen have not protested against horsecars as they did in Rome, tearing up the tracks, mobbing the drivers, and threatening the passengers; neither has the cable superseded horses as a motor power, and the trolley then rendered the cable obsolete.

In short, there never was a horse in Venice, save those bronze ones over the entrance to Saint Mark's, and the one Napoleon rode to the top of the Campanile. But there are lions in Venice—stone lions—you see them at every turn. "Did you ever see a live horse?" asked a ten-year-old boy of me, in Saint Mark's Square ✤ ✤

"Yes," said I, "several times."

"Are they fierce?" he asked after a thoughtful pause. And then I explained that a thousand times as many men are killed by horses every year as by lions.

Four hundred years have made no change in the style of gondolas, or anything else in Venice ✤ The prow of the Venetian gondola made today is of the same height as that prescribed by Tommaso Mocenigo, Doge in the year Fourteen Hundred. The regulated height of the prow is to insure protection for the passengers when going under bridges, but its peculiar halberd shape is a thing not one of the five thousand gondoliers in Venice can explain. If you ask your gondolier he will swear a pious oath, shrug his fine shoulders, and say, "Mon Dieu, Signore! how should I know?—it has always been so."

The ignorance and superstition of the picturesque gondolier, with his fluttering blue hatband and gorgeous sash, are most enchanting. His lack of knowledge is like the ignorance of childhood, when life has neither beginning nor end; when ways and means present no vexatious problems; when if food is not to be had for the simple asking, it can surely be secured by coaxing; when the day is for frolic and play, and the night for dreams and sleep.

But although your gondolier may not be able to read or write, he yet has his preferences in music and art, and possesses definite ideas as to the eternal fitness of things. In Italy, many of the best paintings being in churches, and all the galleries being free on certain days, the common people absorb a goodly modicum of art education without being aware of it. I have heard market-women compare the merits of Tintoretto and Paul Veronese, and stupid indeed is the boat "hooker" in Venice who would not know a "Titian" on sight ❧ ❧

But the chronology of art is all a jumble to this indolent, careless, happy people. These paintings were in the churches when their fathers and mothers were alive, they are here now, and no church has been built in Venice for three hundred years. The history of Venice is nothing to a gondolier. "Why, Signore! how should I know? Venice always has been," explained Enrico, when I asked him how old the city was.

When I hired Enrico I thought he was a youth. He wore such a dandy suit of pure white, and his hatband so exactly matched his sash, that I felt certain I was close upon some tender romance, for surely it was some dark-eyed lacemaker who had embroidered this impossible hatband and evolved the improbable sash!

The exercise of rowing a gondola is of the sort that gives a splendid muscular development. Men who pull oars have round shoulders, but the gondolier does not pull an oar, he pushes it, and as a result has a flat back and brawny chest. Enrico had these, and as he had no nerves to speak of, the passing years had taken small toll. Enrico was sixty ❧

Once he ran alongside another gondola and introduced me to the gondolier, who was his son. They were both of one age. Then one day I went with Enrico to his home—two whitewashed rooms away up under the roof of an old palace on the Rialto—and there met his wife.

Mona Lisa showed age more than Enrico. She had crouched over a little wooden frame making one pattern of lace for thirty years, so her form was bent and her eyesight faulty. Yet she proudly explained that years and years ago she was a model for a painter, and in the Della Salute I could see her picture, posed as Magdalen.

She got fourteen cents a day for her work, and had been at it so long she had no desire to quit. She took great pride in Enrico's white-duck suits and explained to me that she never let him wear one suit more than two days without its being washed and starched; and she always pipeclayed his shoes and carefully inspected him each morning before sending him forth to his day's work. "Men are so careless, you know," she added by way of apology.

There was no furniture in the rooms worth mentioning—Italians do not burden themselves with things—but on the wall I caught sight of a bright-colored unfinished sketch of the Bridge of Sighs. It was little more than an outline, and probably did not represent ten minutes' work, but the lines seemed so firm and sure that I once asked who did it.

¶ "An American did it, Signore, an American painter; he comes here every year; our son is his gondolier and shows him all the best places to paint, and takes him there when the light is good and keeps the people back so the artist can work—you understand? ☙ A shower came up just as his Excellency, the American, began on this, and it got wet and so he gave it to my son and he gave it to me."

"What is the painter's name?" I asked. Enrico could not remember, but Mona Lisa said his name was Signore Hopsmithiziano, or something like that.

There were several little plaster images on the walls, and through the open door that led to the adjoining room I saw a sort of an improvised shrine, with various little votive offerings grouped about an unframed canvas. The picture was a crude attempt at copying that grand central figure in Titian's "Assumption."

"And who painted that?" I asked.

Enrico crossed himself in silence, and Mona Lisa's subdued

voice answered: "Our other son did that. He was only nineteen. He was a mosaicist and was studying to be a painter; he was drowned at the Lido."

The old woman made the sign of the cross, her lips moved, and a single big tear stood on her leathery cheek. I changed the painful subject, and soon found excuse to slip away ✣

That evening as the darkness gathered and twinkling lights began to appear like fireflies, up and down the Grand Canal, I sat in a little balcony of my hotel watching the scene. A serenading party, backing their boats out into the stream, had formed a small blockade, and in the group of gondolas that awaited the unraveling of the tangle I spied Enrico. He had a single passenger, a lady in the inevitable black mantilla, holding in her hands the inevitable fan. A second glance at the lady—and sure enough! it was Mona Lisa ✣

I ran downstairs, stepped out across the moored line of gondolas, took up a hook, and reaching over gently pulled Enrico's gondola over so I could step aboard.

Mona Lisa was crooning a plaintive love-song and her gondolier was coming in occasionally with bars of melo ious bass. I felt guilty for being about to break in upon such a sentimental little scene, and was going to retreat, but Enrico and Mona Lisa spied me and both gave a little cry of surprise and delight.

"Where have you been?" I asked—"you fine old lovers!"

¶ And then they explained that it was a Holy Day and they had been over to the Church of San Giorgio, and were now on their way to Santa Maria de' Frari.

"It is a very special mass, by torchlight, and is for the repose of the soul of Titian, who is buried there. You may never have an opportunity to see such a sight again—come with us," and Enrico held out his strong brown hand.

I stepped aboard, the boats opened out to the left and to the right, and we passed with that peculiar rippling sound, across the water that reflected the lights as of a myriad stars.

# TITIAN

TITIAN was born one hundred years before Rubens, and died just six months before Rubens' birth.

On the one hundred and twenty-second anniversary of the birth of Titian, Rubens knelt at his grave, there in the church of Santa Maria de' Frari, and vowed he would follow in the footsteps of the illustrious master. And the next day he wrote to his mother describing the incident ✤ Thousands of other sentimental and impulsive youth have stood before that little slab of black marble on which is carved the simple legend, "Tiziano Vecellio," and vowed as Rubens did, but out of the throng not one rendered such honor to the master as did the brilliant Fleming. The example of Titian was a lifelong inspiration to Rubens; and to all his pupils he held up Titian as the painter par excellence. In the Rubens studio Titian was the standard by which all art was gauged.

When Rubens returned to Flanders from Italy he carried with him twenty-one pictures done by the hand of the master.
¶ Titian was born at the little village of Cadore, a few miles North of Venice. When ten years of age his father took him down to the city and apprenticed him to a worker in mosaic, the intent of the fond parent probably being to get the youngster out of the way, more than anything else.

The setting together of the little bits of colored glass, according to a pattern supplied, is a task so simple that children can do it about as well as grown folks. They do the work there today just exactly as they did four hundred years ago, when little Tiziano Vecellio came down from Cadore and worked, getting his ears pinched when he got sleepy, or carelessly put in the red glass when he should have used the blue 🙢 🙢

An inscription on a tomb at Beni Hassan, dating from the reign of Osortasen the First, who lived three thousand years before Christ, represents Theban glassblowers at work. I told Enrico of this one day when we were on our way to a glass-factory.

"That's nothing," said Enrico; "it was the glassblowers of Venice who taught them how," and not a ghost of a smile came across his fine, burnt-umber face.

There is a story by Pliny about certain Phenician mariners landing on the shores of a small river in Palestine and making a fire to cook their food, and afterward discovering that the soda and sand under their pots had fused into glass. No one now seriously considers that the first discovery of glass, and for all I know Enrico may be right in his flat statement that the first glass was made at Venice, "for Venice always was."

The art of glassmaking surely goes back to the morning of the world. The glassblower is a classic, like the sower who goes forth to sow, the potter at his wheel, and the grinding of grain with mortar and pestle. Thus, too, the art of the mosaicist—who places bright bits of stone and glass in certain positions so as to form a picture—goes back to the dawn. The exquisite work in mosaic at Pompeii is the first thing that impresses the visitor to that silent city. Much of the work there was done long before the Christian era, and must have then been practised many centuries to bring it to such perfection.

Young Tiziano from Cadore did not like the mere following of a set pattern—he introduced variations of his own, and got his nose tweaked for trying to improve on a good thing. Altogether he seemed to have had a hard time of it there at Messer Zuccato's mosaic-shop.

The painter's art, then as now, preceded the art of the mosaicist, for the picture or design to be made in mosaic is first carefully drawn on paper, and then colored, and the worker in mosaic is supposed simply to follow copy. When you visit the glass-factories of Venice today, you see the painted picture tacked up on the wall before the workmen, who with deft fingers stick the bits of glass into their beds of putty. This scheme of painting a pattern is in order that cheap help can be employed; when it began we do not know, but we do know there was a time when the great artist in mosaic had his design in his head, and materialized it by rightly placing the bits of glass with his own hands, experimenting, selecting and rejecting until the thing was right. But this was before the time of Titian, for when Titian came down to Venice there were painters employed in the shop of Sebastian Zuccato who made the designs for the dunderheads to follow. That is not just the word the painters used to designate the boys and women who placed the bits of glass in position, but it meant the same thing.

The painters thought themselves great folks, and used to make the others wait on them and run errands, serving them as "fags."

But the Vecellio boy did not worship at the shrine of the painters who made the designs. He said he could make as good pictures himself, and still continued to make changes in the designs when he thought they should be made; and once in a dispute between the boy and the maker of a design, the master took sides with the boy. This inflated the lad with his own importance so that shortly after he applied for the position of the quarrelsome designer.

The fine audacity of the youngster so pleased the master that he allowed him to try his hand with the painters a few hours each day. He was getting no wages anyway, only his board, and the kind of board did not cost much, so it did not make much difference.

In Venice at that time there were two painters by the name of Bellini—Gentile and Giovanni, sons of the painter Jacob Bellini, who had brought his boys up in the way they should go. Gian, as the Venetians called the younger brother, was the more noted of the two. Occasionally he made designs for the mosaicists, and this sometimes brought him to the shop where young Titian worked.

The boy got on speaking terms with the great painter, and ran errands back and forth from his studio. When twelve years of age we find him duly installed as a helper at Gian Bellini's studio, with an easel and box of paints all his own.

# TITIAN

THE brightest scholar in the studio of Gian Bellini was a young man by the name of Giorgio, but they called him Giorgione, which being interpreted means George the Great. He was about the age of Titian, and the two became firm friends.

Giorgione was nearly twenty when we first hear of him. He was a handsome fellow—tall, slender, with an olive complexion and dreamy brown eyes. There was a becoming flavor of melancholy in his manner, and more than one gracious dame sought to lure him back to earth, away from his sadness, out of the dream-world in which he lived.

Giorgione was a musician and a poet. He sang his own pieces, playing the accompaniment on a harp. Vasari says he sang his songs, playing his own accompaniment on a flute, but I think this is a mistake.

Into all his work Giorgione infused his own soul—and do you know what the power to do that is? It is genius. To be able to make a statue is little, but to breathe into its nostrils the breath of life—ah! that is something else! The last elusive, undefinable stroke of the brush, that something uniting the spirit of the beholder with the spirit of the artist, so that you feel as he felt when he wrought—that is art ✤ ✤

Burne-Jones is the avatar of Giorgione. He subdues you into silence, and you wait, expecting that one of his tall, soulful dream-women will speak, if you are but worthy—holding your soul in tune.

Giorgione never wrought so well as Burne-Jones, because he lived in a different age—all art is an evolution. Painting is a form of expression, just as language is a form of expression. Every man who writes English is debtor to Shakespeare. Every man who paints and expresses something of that which his soul feels is debtor to Giorgione and Botticelli. But to judge of the greatness of an artist—mind this—you must compare him with his contemporaries, not with those who were before or those who came after. The old masters are valuable, not necessarily for beauty, but because they reveal the evolution of art.

Between Burne-Jones and Giorgione came Botticelli ♪ Botticelli builded on Giorgione, and Burne-Jones builded on Botticelli. Aubrey Beardsley, dead at the age at which Keats died, builded on both, but he perverted their art and put a leer where Burne-Jones placed faith and abiding trust. Aubrey Beardsley got the cue for his hothouse art from one figure in Botticelli's "Spring." I need not state which figure: a glance at the picture and you behold sulphur fumes about the face of one of the women.

Did Aubrey Beardsley infuse his own spirit into his work? Yes, I think he did. Mrs. Jameson says, "There are no successful imitations of Giorgione, neither can there be, for the spirit of the man is in every face he drew, and the people who try to draw like him always leave that out."

¶ There are various pictures in the Louvre, the National Gallery, and the Pinacothek at Munich, signed with Giorgiorne's name, but Mrs. Jameson declares they are not his, "because they do not speak to your soul with that mild, beseeching look of pity." Possibly we should make allowance for Mrs. Jameson's warm praise—other women talked like that when Giorgione was alive.

Giorgione was one of those bright luminaries that dart across our plane of vision and then go out quickly in hopeless night, leaving only the memory of a blinding light. He died at thirty-three, which Disraeli declares is the age at which the world's saviors have usually died—and he names the Redeemer first in a list of twenty who passed out at the age of three and thirty. Disraeli does not say that all those in his list were saviors, for the second name he records is that of Alexander the Great, the list ending with Shelley.

Giorgione died of a broken heart. The girl he loved eloped with his friend, Morta del Feltri, to whom he had proudly introduced her a short time before. It is an old story—it has been played again and again to its Da Rimini finish. The friend introduces the friend, and the lauded virtues of this friend inflames imagination, until love strikes a spark; then soon instead of three we find one—one groping blindly, alone, dazed, stunned, bereft.

The handsome Giorgione pined away, refusing to be comforted. And soon his proud, melancholy soul took its flight from an environment with which he was ever at war, and from a world which he never loved. And Titian was sent for to complete the pictures which he had begun.

Surely, disembodied spirits have no control over mortals, or the soul of Giorgione would have come back and smitten the hand of Titian with palsy.

For a full year before he died Giorgione had not spoken to Titian, although he had seen him daily.

Giorgione had surpassed all artists in Venice. He had a careless, easy, limpid style. But there was decision and surety in his swinging lines, and best of all, a depth of tenderness and pity in his faces that gave to the whole a rich, full and melting harmony.

Giorgione's head touched heaven, and his feet were not always on earth. Titian's feet were always on earth, and his head sometimes touched heaven. Titian was healthy and in love with this old, happy, cruel, sensuous world. He was willing to take his chances anywhere. He had no quarrel with his environment, for did he not stay here a hundred years (lacking half a year), and then die through accident? Of course he liked it. One woman, for him, could make a paradise in which a thousand nightingales sang. And if one particular woman liked some one else better, he just consoled himself with the thought that "there is just as good fish," etc. I will not quote Walt Whitman and say his feet were tenoned and mortised in granite, but they were well planted on the soil—and sometimes mired in clay.

Titian admired Giorgione; he admired him so much that he painted exactly like him—or as nearly as he could.

Titian was a good-looking young man, but he was not handsome like Giorgione. Yet Titian did his best; he patronized Giorgione's tailor, imitated his dreamy, far-away look, used a brush with his left hand, and painted with his thumb. His coloring was the same, and when he got a commission to fresco the ceiling of a church he did it as nearly like Giorgione frescoes as he could.

This kind of thing is not necessarily servile imitation—it is only admiration tipped to t' other side. It is found everywhere in aspiring youth and in every budding artist.

As in the animal kingdom, genius has its prototype. In the National Gallery at London you will see in the Turner Room a "Claude Lorraine" and a "Turner" hung side by side, as provided for in Turner's will. You would swear, were the pictures not labeled, that one hand did them both. When thirty, Turner admired Claude to a slavish degree; but we know there came a time when he bravely set sail on a chartless sea, and left the great Claude Lorraine far astern.

Titian loved Giorgione so well that he even imitated his faults. At first this high compliment was pleasing to Giorgione; then he became indifferent, and finally disgusted. The very sight of Titian gave him a pain.

He avoided his society. He ceased to speak to him when they met, and forbade his friends to mention the name "Titian" in his presence.

It was about this time that Giorgione's ladylove won fame by discarding him in that foolish, fishwife fashion. He called his attendants and instructed them thus: "Do not allow that painter from Cadore—never mind his name— to attend my funeral—you understand?"

Then he turned his face to the wall and died.

In his studio were various pictures partly completed, for it seems to have been his habit to get rest by turning from one piece of work to another. His executors looked at these unfinished canvases in despair. There was only one man in all Venice who could complete them, and that was Titian.

¶ Titian was sent for.

He came, completed the pictures, signed them with the dead man's name, and gave them to the world.

"And," says the veracious Vasari, "they were done just as well, if not better than Giorgione himself could have done them, had he been alive!"

It was absurd of Giorgione to die of a broken heart and let Titian come in, making free with everything in his studio, and complete his work. It was very absurd.

Time is the great avenger—let us wait. Morta del Feltri, the perfidious friend, grew tired of his mistress: their love was so warm it shortly burned itself to ashes—ashes of roses. ¶ Morta deserted the girl, fled from Venice, joined the army, and a javelin plunged through his liver at the Battle of Zara ended his career.

The unhappy young woman, twice a widow, fought off hungry wolves by finding work in a glass-factory, making mosaics at fourteen cents a day. When she was seventy, Titian, aged seventy-five, painted her picture as a beggar-woman.

# TITIAN

THE quality of sentiment that clings about the life of Giorgione seems to forbid a cool, critical view of his work. Byron indited a fine poem to him; and poetic criticism seems for him the proper kind. The glamour of sentiment conceals the real man from our sight. And anyway, it is hardly good manners to approach a saint closely and examine his halo to see whether it be genuine or not. Halos are much more beautiful when seen through the soft, mellow light of distance.

Giorgione's work was mostly in fresco, so but little of it has survived. But of his canvases several surely have that tender, beseeching touch of spirit which stamps the work as great art.

Whether Mrs. Jameson is right in her assumption that all canvases bearing Giorgione's name are spurious which lack that look of pity, is a question. I think Mrs. Jameson is more kind than critical, although my hope is that Renan is correct in his gratuitous statement, "At the Last Great Day men will be judged by women, and the Almighty will merely vise the verdict."

If this be true, all who, like Giorgione, have died for the love of woman will come off lightly.

But the fact is, no man is great all the time. Genius is an exceptional mood even in a genius, and happy is the genius who, like Tennyson, builds a high wall about his house, so he is seen but seldom, and destroys most of his commonplace work ✽ ✽

Ruskin has printed more rubbish than literature—ten times over. I have his complete works, and am sorry to say that instead of confining myself to "Sesame and Lilies" I have foolishly read all the dreary stuff, including statistics, letters to Hobbs and Nobbs, with hot arguments as to who fished the murex up, and long, scathing tirades against the old legal shark who did him out of a hundred pounds. Surely, to be swindled by a lawyer is not so unusual a thing that it is worth recording!

But Ruskin wrote about it, had it put in print, read the proof, and printed the stuff, so no one, no matter how charitably disposed, can arise and zealously declare that this only is genuine, and that spurious. It's all genuine—rubbish, bosh and all.

Titian painted some dreary, commonplace pictures, and he also painted others that must ever be reckoned as among the examples of sublime art that have made the world stronger in its day and proud of what has been.

Titian was essentially a pagan. When he painted Christian subjects he introduced a goodly flavor of the old Greek love of life. Indeed, there is a strong doubt whether the real essence of Christianity was ever known at Venice, except in rare individual cases. It was the spirit of the sea-kings, and not the gentle, loving Christ, that inspired her artists and men of learning. The sensuous glamour of the Orient steeped the walls of San Marco in their rainbow tints, and gave that careless, happy habit to all the Venetian folk. In Titian's time, as today, gay gallants knelt in the churches, and dark, dreamy eyes peeked out from behind mantillas, and the fan spoke a language which all lovers knew. Outside was the strong smell of the sea, and never could a sash be flung open to the azure but there would come floating in on the breeze the gentle tinkle of a guitar.

But Titian, too, as well as Giorgione, infused into his work at times the very breath of life. At the Belle d' Arte at Venice is that grand picture, "The Assumption," which for more than two hundred years was in the Church of Santa Maria de' Frari. When Napoleon appointed a commission to select the paintings in Venice that were considered best worth preserving and protecting, and take them to the Belle d' Arte, this picture was included in the list. It was then removed from its place, where it had so long hung, above the grave of the man who executed it.

I have several large photographs of this picture, showing different portions of it. One of these pictures reveals simply the form of the Virgin. She rises from the earth, caught up in the clouds, the drapery streaming in soft folds, and on the upturned face is a look of love and tenderness and trust, combined with womanly strength, that hushes us into tears.

¶ Surely there is an upward law of gravitation as well as a gravitation that pulls things down. Titian has shown us this. And as he drew over and over again in his pictures the forms and faces of the men and women he knew, so I imagine that this woman was a woman he knew and loved. She is not a far-off, tenuous creature, born of dreams: she is a woman who has lived, suffered, felt, mayhap erred, and now turns to a Power, not herself, eternal in the heavens. Into this picture the artist infused his own exalted spirit, for the mood we behold manifest in others is usually but the reflection of our own spirit.

In some far-off eon, ere this earth-journey began, some woman looked at me that way once, just as Titian has this woman look, with the same melting eyes and half-parted lips, and it made an impression on my soul that subsequent incarnations have not effaced.

I bought the photograph in Venice, at Ongania's, and paid three dollars for it. Then I framed it in simple, unplaned, unstained cedar, and it hangs over my desk now as I write.

¶ When I am tired and things go wrong, and the round blocks all seem to be getting into the square holes, and remembrances of the lawyer who cheated me out of a hundred pounds come stealing like a blight over my spirit, I look up at the face of this woman who is not only angelic but human. I behold the steady upward flight and the tender look of pity, and my soul reaches out, grasping the hem of the garment of Her who we are told was the Mother of God, and with Her I leave the old sordid earth far beneath and go on, and on, and up, and up, and up, until my soaring spirit mingles and communes with the great Infinite.

**ANTHONY VAN DYCK**

ANTHONY VAN DYCK

# ANTHONY VAN DYCK

HIS pieces so with live objects strive,
That both or pictures seem, or both alive.
Nature herself, amaz'd, does doubting stand,
Which is her own and which the painter's hand,
And does attempt the like with less success,
When her own work in twins she would express.
His all-resembling pencil did outpass
The magic imagery of looking-glass.
Nor was his life less perfect than his art.
Nor was his hand less erring than his heart.
There was no false or fading color there,
The figures sweet and well-proportioned were.
  Cowley's "Elegy on Sir Anthony Van Dyck."

# ANTHONY VAN DYCK

VAN DYCK is the most common name in Holland. Its simple inference is that the man lives on the dyke, or near it. In the good old days when villagers never wandered far from home, the appellation was sufficient, and even now it is not especially inconsistent ❧ ❧

In Holland you are quite safe in addressing any man you meet as Van Dyck.

The ancient Brotherhood of Saint Luke, of Antwerp, was always an exclusive affair, but during the years between Fifteen Hundred Ninety-seven and Sixteen Hundred Twenty-three there were twenty-seven artists by the name of Van Dyck upon its membership register. Out of these two dozen and three names, but one interests us.

¶ Anthony Van Dyck was the son of a rich merchant. He was born in the year Fifteen Hundred Ninety-nine — just twenty-two years after the birth of Rubens. Before Anthony was ten years old the name and fame of Rubens illumined all Antwerp, and made it a place of pilgrimage for the faithful lovers of art of Northern Europe.

¶ The success of Rubens fired the ambition of young Van Dyck. His parents fostered his desires, and after he had served an apprenticeship with the artist Van Balen, a place was secured for him in the Rubens studio. For a full year the ambitious Rubens took small notice of the Van Dyck lad, and possibly would not have selected him then as a favorite pupil but for an accident.

Rubens reduced his work to a system. While in his studio he was the incarnation of fire and energy ❧ But at four o'clock each day he dismissed his pupils, locked the doors, and mounting his horse, rode off into the country, five miles and back.

One afternoon, when the master had gone for his usual ride, several of the pupils returned to the studio, wishing to examine a certain picture, and by hook or by crook gained admittance. On an easel was a partly finished canvas, the paint fresh from the hands of the master. The boys examined the work and then began to scuffle—boys of sixteen or seventeen always scuffle when left to themselves. They scuffled so successfully that the easel was upset, and young Van Dyck fell backwards upon the wet canvas, so that the design was transferred to his trousers.

The picture was ruined.

The young men looked upon their work aghast. It meant disgrace for them all.

In despair Van Dyck righted the easel, seized a brush, and began to replace the picture ere it could fade from his memory. His partners in crime looked on with special personal interest and encouraged him with words of lavish praise. He worked to within ten minutes of the time the master was due; and then all made their escape by the window through which they had entered.

# ANTHONY VAN DYCK

The next day, when the class assembled, the pupils were ordered to stand up in line. Then they were catechized individually as to who had replaced the master's picture by one of his own.

All pleaded ignorance until the master reached the blond-haired Van Dyck. The boy made a clean breast of it all, save that he refused to reveal the names of his accomplices.

¶ "Then you painted the picture alone?"

"Yes," came the firm answer that betokened the offender was resolved on standing the consequences.

The master relieved the strained tension by a laugh, and declared that he had only discovered the work was not his own by perceiving that it was a little better than he could do. Accidents are not always unlucky—this advanced young Van Dyck at once to the place of first assistant to Peter Paul Rubens.

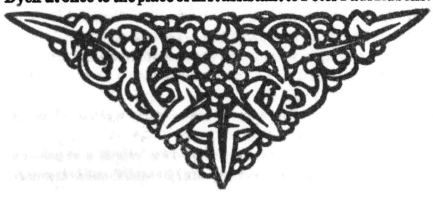

**C**OMMISSIONS were pouring in on Rubens. With him the tide was at flood. He had been down to Paris and had returned in high spirits with orders to complete that extensive set of pictures for Marie De Medici; he also had commissions from various churches; and would-be sitters for portraits waited in his parlors, quarreling about which should have first place.

Van Dyck, his trusted first lieutenant, lived in his house. The younger man had all the dash, energy and ambition of the older one. He caught the spirit of the master, and so great was his skill that he painted in a way that thoroughly deceived the patrons; they could not tell whether Rubens or Van Dyck had done the work.

This was very pleasing to Rubens. But when Van Dyck began sending out pictures on his own account, properly signed, and people said they were equal to those of Rubens, if not better, Rubens shrugged his shoulders.

There was as little jealousy in the composition of Peter Paul Rubens as in any artistic man we can name; but to declare that he was incapable of jealousy, as a few of his o'er-zealous defenders did, is to apply the whitewash. The artistic temperament is essentially feminine, and jealousy is one of its inherent attributes. Of course there are all degrees of jealousy but the woman who can sit serenely by and behold her charms ignored for those of another, by one who yesterday sat at her feet making ballad to her eyebrow and sighing like a furnace, does not exist on the planet called Earth.

The artist, in any line, craves praise, and demands applause as his lawful right; and the pupil who in excellence approaches him, pays him a compliment that warms the cockles of his heart. But let a pupil once equal him and the pupil's name is anathema. I can not conceive of any man born of woman who would not detest another man who looked like him, acted like him, and did difficult things just as well. Such a one robs us of our personality, and personality is all there is of us.

The germ of jealousy in Rubens' nature had never been developed. He dallied with no "culture-beds," and the thought that any one could ever really equal him had never entered his mind. His conscious sense of power kept his head high above the miasma of fear.

But now a contract for certain portraits that were to come from the Rubens studio had been drawn up by the Jesuit Brothers, and in the contract was inserted a clause to the effect that Van Dyck should work on each one of the pictures.

¶ "Pray you," said Rubens, "to which Van Dyck do you refer? There are many of the name in Antwerp."

The jealousy germ had begun to develop.

And about this time Van Dyck was busying himself as understudy, by making love to Rubens' wife. Rubens was a score of years older than his pupil, and Isabella was somewhere between the two—say ten years older than Van Dyck, but that is nothing! These first fierce flames that burn in the heart of youth are very apt to be for some fair dame much older than himself. No psychologist has ever yet just fathomed the problem, and I am sure it is too deep for me—I give it up. And yet the fact remains, for how about Doctor Samuel Johnson—and did not our own Robert Louis fall desperately in love with a woman sixteen years his senior? Aye, and married her, too, first asking her husband's consent, and furtherance also being supplied by the ex-husband giving the bride away at the altar. At least, we have been told so.

¶ Were this sketch a catalog, a dozen notable instances could be given in which very young men have been struck hard by women old enough to have nursed them as babes.

¶ Van Dyck loved Isabella Rubens ardently. He grew restless, feverish, lost appetite and sighed at her with lackluster eye across the dinner-table. Rubens knew of it all, and smiled a grim, sickly smile.

"I, too, love every woman who sits to me for a portrait. He'll get over it," said the master. "It all began when I allowed him to paint her picture."

Busy men of forty, with ambitions, are not troubled by Anthony Hope's interrogation. They glibly answer, "No, no, love is not all—it's only a small part of life—simply incidental!"

But Van Dyck continued to sigh, and all of his spare time was taken up in painting pictures of the matronly Isabella. He managed to work even in spite of loss of appetite; and sitters sometimes called at the studio and asked for "Master Van Dyck," whereas before there was only one master in the whole domain.

Rubens grew aweary.

He was too generous to think of crushing Van Dyck, and too wise to attempt it. To cast him out and recognize him openly as a rival would be to acknowledge his power. A man with less sense would have kicked the lovesick swain

# ANTHONY VAN DYCK

into the street. Rubens was a true diplomat. He decided to get rid of Van Dyck and do it in a way that would cause no scandal, and at the same time be for the good of the young man ✸ ✸

He took Van Dyck into his private office and counseled with him calmly, explaining to him how hopeless must be his love for Isabella. He further succeeded in convincing the youth that a few years in Italy would add the capsheaf to his talent. Without Italy he could not hope to win all; with Italy all doors would open at his touch.

Then he led him to his stable and presented him with his best saddle-horse, and urged immediate departure for a wider field and pastures new.

A few days later the handsome Van Dyck—with a goodly purse of gold, passports complete, and saddlebags well filled with various letters of introduction to Rubens' Italian friends —followed by a cart filled with his belongings, started gaily away, bound for the land where art had its birth.

"With Italy—with Italy I can win all!" he kept repeating to himself as he turned his horse's head to the South.

THE first day's ride took the artistic traveler to the little village of Saventhem, five miles from Brussels. Here he turned aside long enough to say good-by to a fair young lady, Anna Van Ophem by name, whom he had met a few months before at Antwerp.

He rode across the broad pasture, entered the long lane lined with poplars, and followed on to the spacious old stone mansion in the grove of trees.

Anna herself saw him coming and came out to meet him. They had not been so very well acquainted, but the warmth of a greeting all depends upon where it takes place. It was lonely for the beautiful girl there in the country: she welcomed the handsome young painter-man as though he were a long-lost brother, and proudly introduced him to her parents ✄ ✄

Instead of a mere call he was urged to put up his horse and remain over night; and a servant was sent out to find the man who drove the cart with the painter's belongings, and make him comfortable.

The painter decided that he would remain over night and make an early start on the morrow.

And it was so agreed.

There was music in the evening, and pleasant converse until a late hour, for the guest must sit up and see the moon rise across the meadow—it would make such a charming subject for a picture!

So they sat up to see the moon rise across the meadow.

At breakfast the next morning there was a little banter on the subject of painting. Could not the distinguished painter remain over one day and give his hosts a taste of his quality?

¶ "I surely will if the fair Anna will sit for her portrait!" he courteously replied.

The fair Anna consented.

The servant who drove the cart had gotten on good terms with the servants of the household, and was being initiated into the mysteries of making Dutch cheese.

Meanwhile the master had improvised a studio and was painting the portrait of the charming Anna.

After working two whole days he destroyed the canvas because the picture was not keyed right, and started afresh. This picture was fairish good, but his desire now was to paint the beautiful Anna as the Madonna.

Van Dyck's affections having been ruthlessly uprooted but a few days before, the tendrils very naturally clung to the first object that presented itself—and this of course was the intelligent and patient sitter, aged nineteen last June.

If Rubens could not paint the picture of a lady without falling in love with her, what should be expected of his best pupil, Van Dyck?

Pygmalion loved into life the cold marble which his hand had shaped, and thus did Van Dyck love his pictures into being. All portrait painters are sociable—they have to be in order to get acquainted with the subject. The best portrait-painter in America talks like a windmill as he works, and tries a whole set round of little jokes, and dry asides and trite aphorisms on the sitter, meanwhile cautiously noting the effect. For of course so long as a sitter is coldly self-conscious, and fully mindful that he is "being took," his countenance is as stiff, awkward, and constrained as that of a farmer at a dinner-party. Hence the task devolves on the portrait artist to bring out, by the magic of his presence, the nature of the subject. "In order to paint a truly correct likeness, you must know your sitter thoroughly," said Van Dyck.

The gracious Rubens prided himself on his ability in this line. He would often spend half an hour busily mending a brush or mixing paints, talking the while, but only waiting for the icy mood of the sitter to thaw. Then he would arrange the raiment of his patron, sometimes redress the hair, especially of his lady patrons, and once we know he kissed the cheek of the Duchess of Mantua, "so as to dispel her distant look."

I know a portrait artist in Albany who is said to occasionally salute his lady customers by the same token, and if they protest he simply explains to them that it was all in the interest of art—in other words, artifice for art's sake.

After three days at the charming old country-seat at Saventhem, Van Dyck called his servant and told him to take the shoes off of the saddle-horse, and turn it and the cart-horse loose in the pasture. He had decided to remain and paint a picture for the village church.

And it was so done.

The pictures that Van Dyck then painted are there now in the same old ivy-grown, moss-covered church at Saventhem. The next time you are in Brussels it will pay you to walk out and see them.

One of the pictures is called "Saint Martin Dividing His

# ANTHONY VAN DYCK

Cloak With Two Beggars." The Saint is modestly represented by Van Dyck himself, seated astride the beautiful horse that Rubens gave him.

The other picture is "The Holy Family," in which the fair Anna posed for the Virgin, and her parents and kinsmen are grouped around her as the Magi and attendants.

Both pictures reveal the true Van Dyck touch, and are highly prized by the people of the village and the good priests of the church. Each night a priest carries in a cot and sleeps in the chancel to see that these priceless works of art are protected from harm. When you go there to see them, give the cowled attendant a franc and he will unfold the tale, not just as I have written it, but substantially. He will tell you that Van Dyck stopped here on his way to Italy and painted these pictures as a pious offering to God, and what boots it after all!

More than once have the village peasants collected, armed with scythes, hoes and pitchforks, to protect these sacred pictures from vandalism on the part of lustful collectors or marauding bands of soldiers.

In Eighteen Hundred Fourteen, a detachment of French soldiers killed a dozen of the villagers, and a priest fell fighting for these treasures on the sacred threshold, stabbed to his death ✤ Then the vandals tramped over the dead bodies, entered the church, and cut from its frame Van Dyck's "Holy Family" and carried the picture off to Paris. But after Napoleon had gotten his Waterloo (only an hour's horseback ride from Saventhem), the picture was restored to the villagers on order of the Convention.

Rubens waited expectantly, thinking to have news from his brilliant pupil in Italy. He waited a month. Two months passed, and still no word. After three months a citizen reported that the day before he had seen Van Dyck, aided by a young woman, putting up a picture in the village church at Saventhem. ¶ Rubens saddled his horse and rode down there. He found Van Dyck and his lady-love sitting hand in hand on a mossy bank, in a leafy grove, listening to the song of a titmouse. Rubens did not chide the young man; he merely took him one side and told him that he had stayed long enough, and "beyond the Alps lies Italy." He also suggested that Anthony Van Dyck could not afford to follow the example of his illustrious Roman namesake who went down into Egypt and found things so softly luxurious that he forgot home, friends, country—all! To remain at Saventhem would be death to his art—he must have before him the example of the masters.

Van Dyck said he would think about it; and Rubens took a look at his old saddle-horse rolling in the pasture or wading knee-deep in clover, and rode back home.

In a few days he sent Chevaller Nanni down to the country-seat at Saventhem, to tell Van Dyck that he was on his way to Italy and that Van Dyck had better accompany him.

Van Dyck concluded to go. He made tearful promises to his beautiful Anna that he would return for her in a year.

And so the servant, who had become an expert in the making of Dutch cheese, caught the horses out of the pasture, and having rebroken them, the cavalcade started Southward in good sooth.

# ANTHONY VAN DYCK

**I**T was four years before Van Dyck returned. He visited Milan, Florence, Verona, Mantua, Venice and Rome, and made himself familiar with the works of the masters. Everywhere he was showered with attention, and the fact that he was the friend and protege of Rubens won him admittance into the palaces of the nobles.

The four years in Italy widened his outlook and transformed him from a merely handsome youth into a man of dignity and poise.

Great was his relief when he returned to Antwerp to hear that the pretty Anna Van Ophem of Saventhem had been married three years before to a worthy wine merchant of Brussels, and was now the proud mother of two handsome boys ✤ ✤

Great was the welcome that Van Dyck received at Antwerp; and in it all the gracious Rubens joined. But there was one face the returned traveler missed: Isabella had died the year before.

The mere fact that a man has been away for several years studying his profession gives him a decided prestige when he returns. Van Dyck, fresh from Italy, exuberant with life and energy, became at once the vogue.

He opened a studio, following the same lines that Rubens had, and several churches gave him orders for extensive altarpieces ✤ ✤

Antwerp prided herself on being an artistic center. Buyers from England now and then appeared, and several of Rubens' pictures had been taken to London to decorate the houses and halls of royalty.

Portrait-painting is the first form of art that appeals to a rude and uncultivated people. To reproduce the image of a living man in stone, or to show a likeness of his face in paint, is calculated to give a thrill even to a savage. There is something mysterious in the art, and the desire to catch the shadow ere the substance fades is strong in the human heart. One reason that sacred art was so well encouraged in the Middle Ages was because the faces portrayed were reproductions of living men and women. This lent an intense personal interest in the work, and insured its fostering care. Callous indeed was the noble who would not pay good coin to have himself shown as Saint Paul, or his enemy as Judas. In fact, "Judas Receiving the Thirty Pieces of Silver" was a very common subject, and the "Judas" shown was usually some politician who had given offense.

In Sixteen Hundred Twenty-eight, England had not yet developed an art-school of her own. All her art was an importation, for although some fine pictures had been produced in England, they were all the work of foreigners —men who had been brought over from the Continent.

Henry the Eighth had offered Raphael a princely sum if he would come to London and work for a single year. Raphael, however, could not be spared from Italy to do work for "the barbarians," and so he sent his pupil, Luca Penni. Bluff old Hans Holbein also abode in England and drew a goodly pension from the State.

During the reign of Mary and her Spanish husband, Philip, several pictures by Titian arrived in London, via Madrid. Then, too, there were various copies of pictures by Paul

# ANTHONY VAN DYCK

Veronese, Murillo and Velasquez that long passed for original, because the copyist had faithfully placed the great artist's trademark in the proper place.

Queen Elizabeth held averages good by encouraging neither art nor matrimony—whereas her father had set her the example of being a liberal patron of both. If Elizabeth never discovered Shakespeare, how could she be expected to know Raphael?

About Sixteen Hundred Twenty, the year the "Mayflower" sailed, Paul Vensomer, Cornelis Jannsen and Daniel Mytens went over to England from the Netherlands and quickly made fortunes by painting portraits for the nobility. This was the first of that peculiar rage for having a hall filled with ancestors. The artists just named painted pictures of people long gone hence, simply from verbal descriptions, and warranted the likeness to give satisfaction.

Oh, the Dutch are a thrifty folk!

James the First had no special eye for beauty—no more than Elizabeth had—but a few of his nobles were intent on providing posterity with handsome ancestors, and so the portrait-painter flourished.

An important move in the cause of literature was made by King James when he placed Sir Walter Raleigh in the Tower; for Raleigh's best contributions to letters were made during those thirteen years when he was alone, with the world locked out. And when his mind began to lose its flash, the King wisely put a quietus on all danger of an impaired output by cutting off the author's head.

Still, there was no general public interest in art until the generous Charles appeared upon the scene. Charles was an elegant scholar and prided himself on being able to turn a sonnet or paint a picture; and the only reason, he explained, why he did not devote all his time to literature and art was because the State must be preserved. He could hire men to paint, but where could one be found who could govern?

Charles had purchased several of Rubens' pieces, and these had attracted much attention in London. Receptions were given where crowds surged and clamored and fought, just to get a look at the marvelous painting of the wonderful Fleming. Such gorgeous skill in color had never before been seen in England ✤ ✤

Charles knighted Rubens and did his best to make him a permanent attache of his Court; but Rubens had too many interests of a financial and political nature at home to allow himself to be drawn away from his beloved Antwerp.

But now he had a rival—the only real rival he had ever known. Van Dyck was making head. The rival was younger, handsomer, and had such a blandishing tongue and silken manner that the crowd began to call his name and declare he was greater than Cæsar.

Yet Rubens showed not a sign of displeasure on his fine face—he bowed and smiled and agreed with the garrulous critics when they smote the table and declared that all of Van Dyck's Madonnas really winked.

He bided his time.

And it soon came, for the agent of Lord Arundel, that great Mæcenas of the polite arts, came over to Flanders to secure treasures, and of course called on Rubens.

# ANTHONY VAN DYCK

And Rubens talked only of Van Dyck—the marvelous Van Dyck ♣ ♣

The agent secured several copies of Van Dyck's work, and went back to England, telling of all that Rubens had told him, with a little additional coloring washed in by his own warm imagination.

To discover a genius is next to being one yourself. Lord Arundel felt that all he had heard of Van Dyck must be true, and when he went to the King and told him of the prodigy he had found, the King's zeal was warm as that of the agent, for does not the "messianic instinct" always live?

¶ This man must be secured at any cost. They had failed to secure Rubens, but the younger man had no family ties, no special property interests, neither was he pledged to his home government as was Rubens.

Straightway the King of England dispatched a messenger urging Anthony Van Dyck to come over to England. The promised rewards and honors were too great for the proud and ambitious painter to refuse. He started for England.

VAN DYCK was short in stature but of a very compact build. He carried the crown of his head high, his chin in, and his chest out. His name is another added to that list of big-little men who had personality plus, and whose presence filled a room. Cæsar, Napoleon, Lord Macaulay, Aaron Burr and that other little man with whom Burr's name is inseparably linked, belong to the same type. These little men with such dynamic force that they can do the thinking for a race are those who have swerved the old world out of her ruts—whether for good or ill is not the question here.

When you find one of these big-little men, if he does not stalk through society a conquering Don Juan it is because we still live in an age of miracles.

Women fed on Van Dyck's smile, and pined when he did not deign to notice them. He was royal in all his tastes—his manner was regal, and so proud was his step that when he passed forbidden lines, sentinels and servants saluted and made way, never daring to ask him for card, passport or countersign.

He gloried in his power and worked it to its farthest limit.
¶ Unlike Rembrandt, he never painted beggars; nor did he ever stoop as Titian did when he pictured his old mother as a peasant woman at market, in that gem of the Belle d' Arte at Venice; nor did he ever reveal on his canvas wrinkled, weather-worn old sailors, as did Velasquez.

He pictured only royalty, and managed, in all his portraits, to put a look of leisure and culture and quiet good breeding into the face, whether it was in the original or not. In fact, he fused into every picture that he painted a goodly modicum of his own spirit. You can always tell a Van Dyck portrait; there is in the face a self-sufficiency, a something that speaks of "divine right"—not of arrogance, for arrogance and assumption reveal a truth which man is trying to hide, and that is that his position is a new acquirement. Van Dyck's people are all to the manor born.

He was thirty-three years old when he arrived in England.
¶ King Charles furnished the painter a house at Blackfriars, fronting the Thames, to insure a good light, and gave him a Summer residence in Kent. All his expenses were paid by the State, and as his tastes were regal the demands on the public exchequer were not small. His title was, "Principal Painter in Ordinary to the King and Queen of England."
¶ Van Dyck had worked so long with Rubens that he knew how to use 'prentice talent. He studied by a system and turned off a prodigious number of canvases. The expert can at once tell a picture painted by Van Dyck during his career in England: it lacks the care and finish that was shown in his earlier years. Yet there is a subtle sweep and strength in it all that reveals the personality of the artist.

Twenty-two pictures he painted of King Charles that we can trace. These were usually sent away as presents. And it is believed that in the seven years Van Dyck lived in England he painted nearly one thousand portraits.

The courtly manner and chivalrous refinement of the Fleming made him a prime favorite of Charles. He was even more kingly than the King.

In less than three months after he arrived in England

Charles publicly knighted him, and placed about his neck a chain of gold to which was attached a locket, set with diamonds, containing a picture of the King.

A record of Van Dyck's affairs of the heart would fill a book. His old habit of falling in love with every lady patron grew upon him. His reputation went abroad, and his custom of thawing the social ice by talking soft nonsense to the lady on the sitter's throne, while it repelled some allured others.

¶ At last Charles grew nettled and said that to paint Lady Digby as "The Virgin" might be all right, and even to turn around and picture her as "Susanna at the Bath" was not necessarily out of place, but to show Margaret Lemon, Anne Carlisle and Catherine Wotton as "The Three Graces" was surely bad taste. And furthermore, when these same women were shown as "Psyche," "Diana" and the "Madonna" —just as it happened—it was really too much!

In fact, the painter must get married; and the King and Queen selected for him a wife in the person of a Scottish beauty, Maria Ruthven.

Had this proposition come a few years before, the proud painter would have flouted it. But things were changed. Twinges of gout and sharp touches of sciatica backed up the King's argument that to reform were the part of wisdom. Van Dyck's manly shape was tending to embonpoint: he had evolved a double chin, the hair on his head was rather seldom, and he could no longer run upstairs three steps at a time. Yes, he would get married, live the life of a staid, respectable citizen, and paint only religious subjects. Society was nothing to him—he would give it up entirely ❧ ❧

And so Sir Anthony Van Dyck was married to Maria Ruthven, at Saint Paul's Cathedral, and the King gave the bride away, ceremonially and in fact.

Sir Anthony's gout grew worse, and after some months the rheumatism took an inflammatory turn. Other complications entered, which we would now call Bright's Disease—that peculiar complaint of which poor men stand in little danger.

¶ The King offered the Royal Physician a bonus of five hundred pounds if he would cure Van Dyck: but if he had threatened to kill the doctor if the patient died, just as did the Greek friends of Byron, when the poet was ill at Rome, it would have made no difference.

A year after his marriage, and on the day that Maria Ruthven gave birth to a child, Anthony Van Dyck died, aged forty years. Rubens had died but a few months before.

The fair Scottish wife did not care to retain her illustrious name at the expense of loneliness, and so shortly married again. Whom she married matters little, since it would require a search-warrant to unearth even the man's name, so dead is he. But inasmuch as the brilliant Helena Fourment, second wife of Rubens, whose picture was so often painted by her artist-husband, married again, why should n't Madame Van Dyck follow the example?

It is barely possible that Charles Lamb was right when he declared that no woman married to a genius ever believed her husband to be one. We know that the wife of Edmund Spenser became the Faery Queen of another soon after his demise, and whenever Spenser was praised in her presence she put on a look that plainly said, "I could a tale unfold."

¶ My own opinion is that a genius makes a very bad husband. And further, I have no faith in that specious plea, "A woman who marries a second time confers upon her first husband the highest compliment, for her action implies that she was so happy in her first love that she is more than willing to try it again."

I think the reverse is more apt to be the truth, and that the woman who has been sorely disappointed in her first marriage is anxious to try the great experiment over again, in order if possible to secure that bliss which every daughter of Eve feels is her rightful due.

Maria Ruthven lived to rear a goodly brood of children, and Samuel Pepys records that she used to send a sort o' creepy feeling down the backs of callers by innocently introducing her children thus: "This is my eldest daughter, whose father was Sir Anthony Van Dyck, of whom you have doubtless heard; and these others are my children by my present husband, Sergeant Nobody."

Van Dyck's remains are buried in Saint Paul's Cathedral. A very fine monument, near the grave of Turner, marks the spot; but his best monument is in the examples of his work that are to be found in every great art-gallery of the world.

SO HERE ENDETH BOOK ONE OF EMINENT PAINTERS, THE SAME BEING ONE OF THE SERIES OF LITTLE JOURNEYS, AS WRITTEN BY ELBERT HUBBARD: THE BORDERS AND INITIALS BEING DESIGNED BY ROYCROFT ARTISTS, AND THE WHOLE DONE INTO A PRINTED VOLUME BY THE ROYCROFTERS, AT THEIR SHOP, WHICH IS IN EAST AURORA, ERIE COUNTY, NEW YORK STATE, IN THE YEAR MCMXI

CPSIA information can be obtained
at www.ICGtesting.com
Printed in the USA
BVHW02s2144170118
505621BV00012B/138/P